To Sara, who made me a dad.

Celebrating 47 Years
2325 Third Street, Suite 344
San Francisco, California 94107
www.potreroview.net

Copyright © 2017 The Potrero View
Illustrations by TJ Frizs
Book design by Simon Stahl

Printed and bound in the USA.

1 2 3 4 5

The Daddy Handbook

Steven Moss

Contents

Preface: Father's Day

"You're going to have three kids," seven-year-old Sara announced, after examining the number of lines on my wrist. I tried not to wince as my daughter then held up her arm for me to predict her child-bearing fortune.

I came to fatherhood at an age that's considered late. Sara was born when I was 40 – 13 years older than average for a first-time father. By the standards of having children, I was already over-the-hill: fertility rates peak by the time a man reaches his mid-30s, and fall from there.

Still, while I may be older, the experiences I've had being a dad are much closer to today's 20-something pops than my 1960s-era father. Dads now spend almost three times as many hours with their children – and more than twice as much time on housework – than their fathers did. I'm not in the same league as stay-at-home dads, of which there may be in the neighborhood of 1.4 million. But most modern fathers are probably like me. We've dived into the enterprise head first, with a deep commitment to raising our children, but with minimal training and incomplete role models.

Except from a biological perspective, becoming a dad isn't like turning on a light switch. It's akin to making tea: a sudden splash into boiling water, followed by a slow transformation. This is the story of that transformation; how I raised my daughter and my daughter raised me. In many ways, it's every dad's story. Though the characters change, and the plot line may take a different trajectory, it's a tale that most fathers can, and should, tell, and will be encouraged to do so at the end of this book. And a quick caution: parts of this book are funny, parts are sad, and parts are neither. Just like life.

Handbook Tips: So You Want to Become a Father...or do you?
▸ *Sex = Life*. Most single men only loosely connect sex with any other outcome than going to sleep afterwards, or, during the *Mad Men* days, having a post-coital cigarette. (I'm not sure what the current practice is; chewing on a slab of Nicorette wouldn't seem to work). Here's a little known fact: sex can create a baby; after a baby there's very little sex. Either there's some evolutionary

advantage to refocusing male sexual energy elsewhere after becoming a father, or God is laughing at us.

▸ *Life = Love.* Setting aside any conclusions you came to related to (1), go ahead, have a baby. In fact, why stop at one; go for two, or even three. There are downsides to the enterprise – someone else in the house with a shorter attention span than you; being forced to share your stuff; you and your things will get drooled on, crumpled, or broken – but it beats the alternative.

▸ *Make a commitment.* Once the baby pops out she'll be with you for a lifetime; it's good to teach her something. I started taking Sara to swimming lessons when she turned three, driving 30 miles from San Francisco to Half Moon Bay once a week for almost two years. Today Sara swims like a mermaid, and I get the credit.

▸ *Grow up.* There's plenty of time to stay in suspended adolescence, messing around with women, sports, travel, and technology. Feel free to take all the time you need; then, by faith or circumstance, stop acting like a boy.

Small Size, Big Entrance

"You're going to have your baby today," our heavily tattooed and pierced waiter said, as he placed a platter of vegetarian *Huevos Rancheros* in front of Debbie. We were at our favorite neighborhood diner, a place so small that the grill was one step away from our table, and within two strides of the entrance.

"Why do you say that?" Debbie asked.

"Well, look at you," he cried, gesturing towards Debbie's bulging middle, which out-competed her flowing red hair for attention. "And our *Huevos* always triggers birth. Something about the spices." He pivoted away to take another customer's order.

"You can't have the baby today," I said, glancing at the departing waiter; had he added another nose piercing? "We have tickets to the theater tonight. Plus we gotta pick-up the car." Debbie smiled like the Mona Lisa, and tucked into her eggs.

It was a beautiful San Francisco day. Warm enough for short sleeves; crisp enough to see Mount Diablo from the City. As we drove across the Bay Bridge to a Volvo dealership in Oakland, where we'd arranged to lease a car, Debbie started to squirm in her seat.

"Something's not right," she said, through clenched teeth.

"Maybe it's the eggs," I said.

"No," she grimaced. "Contractions."

"Are you okay?"

"Yes," she breathed out, the contraction having passed. "I'm fine."

At the dealership a buttoned-down, baby-faced salesperson showed us our car, enthusiastically explaining its features. As we signed the paperwork, Debbie suddenly clutched her stomach.

"I think I'm going into labor!" she exclaimed.

The salesperson and I looked at one another, eyes round.

"We gotta go," I said, nervously. "Let's get to the hospital."

I ushered Debbie out of the showroom into my convertible SAAB. The salesperson followed behind, wringing his hands, assuring us that he'd arrange to have the car delivered to us. Debbie got in. She writhed in her seat, arching her back, pushing herself up from the chair. I put the top down; no need to waste a rare sunshiny day.

The Bay Bridge was packed with day-tripping tourists, drawn to San Francisco's non-foggy pleasures. Cars from multiple directions funneled into the toll plaza, creating a bottleneck that overflowed back towards Berkeley and Oakland. Debbie's moans were getting sharper; more frequent. To my right I saw that the bus-only lane was empty. I pulled into it, and started to accelerate. Behind me, a Highway Patrol officer turned on his siren, indicating that I should pull over.

"You're driving in a designated bus lane," said the officer through the driver's side window. His uniform was so crisp it looked like it could have walked off on its own. "Driver's license and insurance, please."

"My wife's in labor," I said, without reaching for my wallet. "We need to get to the hospital."

Next to me Debbie squirmed in pain.

"If you're wife is really in labor she should be in an ambulance," he responded, stone faced.

"I don't want an ambulance! I just wanna get to the hospital. I don't want an ambulance," Debbie cried.

"You either sit in traffic, in the correct lane, or I'm calling an ambulance," he turned on his heels, and strode back to his patrol car.

I scanned the traffic clogged around us. I looked at Debbie, who was arching her back, pushing up on the seat, in pain. "Screw this," I said, and pulled away into the bus lane. The cop didn't follow.

Once we got past the toll gates, traffic lightened.

At the hospital Debbie was whisked into a delivery room. A 20-something resident with thick black hair and a shiny smile came by to check her progress. He took Debbie's pulse, and measured her round stomach with his hands.

"Everything looks good," he grinned. "I'd say you're having a seven pound baby."

We waited. Debbie shifted on the crinkly blue hospital paper covering the bed, regularly wincing. I tried to be useful, and failed. We listened to the whirl of hospital sounds outside our room; the beeping of heart machines, the rubbery clop of nurses' shoes; patients being ushered to areas behind thin curtains.

As the tempo of Debbie's pain worsened – complete with excruciating back spasms – a nurse wheeled in what looked like a saline solution stand to give her an epidural.

"Bring it on!" Debbie grimaced. "Enough of this natural child birth."

A few hours later Sara decided she was ready to come out. As she slid into the world, the nurses' and doctors' smiles turned into frowns. She was alarmingly small for a full-term baby: four pounds, 11 ounces. Seeing the expressions on the medical personnel's faces, Debbie and I looked at one another with concern.

"Is something wrong?" she mouthed to me.

A code was called, and the room became crowded with medical personnel, jostling me to the back of the small space. A nurse placed Sara in a mobile incubator, and wheeled her off to the intensive pediatric care unit. Debbie waved at me to follow.

As I trailed after the nurse pushing Sara away I glanced back at my wife. She was frowning slightly, tears at the edges of her eyes, looking like she'd lost something.

It took us less than a minute to get to the ICU, where the nurse parked Sara's incubator, locked the wheels, and strode away, leaving me alone with my daughter. The room was like an aquarium, with dimmed lights and plastic bubbles holding what looked like outsized versions of sea monkeys. I sat next to Sara. She was small and wrinkly, lying on her back and waving her arms around like seaweed slow-dancing underwater. She looked perfect to me. I glanced at the incubator across the narrow hall, where a much smaller baby was hooked up to multiple tiny tubes. I prayed.

Two years before Sara appeared, when Debbie was five months into a pregnancy, we lost what would have been our first son. Debbie had just finished giving a lecture at a local university when her water broke. She drove herself to the hospital, was rushed into the emergency room, and hooked-up to an ultra-sound. She saw the fetus wriggling in distress. Then he died.

I arrived shortly afterwards. For the next several hours Debbie labored to give birth to a still-born. He came out tiny and shriveled, clearly on his way to becoming a fully functioning person, but not there yet. Debbie held him and kissed him goodbye. I couldn't do either.

Despite that loss I was certain that Sara was going to

be fine. Not because I knew anything about her condition, or why she was born so small. While I was middle aged, I was still pushed along by the hubris of youth, where – even though experience had taught me otherwise – bad things happened to other people. The prayer I said to myself wasn't so much desperate, like I thought Sara faced serious issues. It was more akin to the whispered assurances a teenage boy would tell himself just before he jumped from a high boulder into a cold mountain stream.

It felt much longer, but within an hour Sara was released from ICU. A nurse wheeled her back to Debbie, who quickly reached for her, cradling the tiny, mewling, body in her relieved arms for the first time. The doctor asked us to stay at the hospital for an additional night or two for observation.

"What's wrong with Sara?" my mother demanded, her brow furrowed, when she visited. "They don't keep babies longer than they have to unless there's something wrong."

"She's just small." I said. "She's fine."

The doctors guessed that Sara had suffered from intrauterine growth restriction, most likely because the umbilical cord connecting her to nourishment from Debbie was too narrow. She hadn't gotten enough to eat. Though small, she was otherwise healthy. Her growth would need to be monitored, but, they said, she'd likely catch up over time.

Handbook Tips: Bad Things Will Happen
▸ Bad things will happen; it's how you deal with them that matters.

▸ Prayer may or may not work, but it's a lot quieter than cursing, less harmful than smoking, and the people around you will respect it.

▸ Size doesn't matter: small babies cry just as loudly as big ones.

▸ There seems to be an infinite number of ways that you can accidentally kill your baby: choking, falling off their changing table, drowning in the bathtub. Like many new parents, for the first year of her life I checked to see whether Sara was still breathing when she slept. Fortunately, she survived my near-smothering attention.

▸ Once you get past those early years, you can pretty much breathe easy. Adolescents and teenagers face far fewer physical hazards, though emotional ones abound. That is until roughly high school, when you'll have to deal with driving, drinking, and drugs. In the meantime, enjoy your kid's childhood as much as they do!

Entertaining Your Baby

Babies remember nothing. Their short-term memory lasts as long as a soap bubble, which pops and disappears almost immediately after it's formed. This weakness makes them well-known suckers for visual humor, of the peak-a-boo variety.

When my nephew, Asa, was about 18-months old, he started fussing during a religious service my extended family was attending. Looking for just such an opportunity to escape the repetitive chanting, I carried him out of the synagogue, onto the street, in search of something engaging to do. I spotted a row of mechanical parking meters and strolled over, thinking that he might be amused by the whirling of the knob, and the clicking sound made by the purchase of time.

With a magician's flare, I produced a quarter from my pocket, waved it in front of him, slid it into the coin slot, and twisted the knob. The quarter disappeared into the machine, but, without changing the meter time, it immediately popped out of a return slot. Startled, I grabbed the coin as it flew towards the pavement. Asa shrieked with laughter.

I grinned at him. My trick had been a hit, though mostly because of the unexpectedly broken meter. Even I was amused. Asa quickly settled back into a look of edgy boredom. I held the coin up to him again, slid it back into the meter, and twisted the knob. As it flew from the return slot Asa broke into a whole body giggle. I stuck the coin in again; more liquid laughter from Asa. I repeated the trick a half-dozen times. Each time Asa was delighted, as if he'd just seen the funniest thing in his life.

As far as I could tell, I could've stood at that meter, twisted the knob, and sparked Asa's uninhibited laughter, forever. But I do have short-term memory. I got bored. After one more hilarious spin cycle, I carried Asa back into the crowded synagogue and sat down. He fell asleep in my arms in a satisfied stupor.

Mindful of this experience, when Sara was fussing at around the same age I devised a new trick. I stuffed a tissue in my hand, and pretended to sneeze, blowing the soft paper into the air. Sara burst out laughing. I did it again; same results. I tried it a third time, but the tissue didn't fly quite as high. Sara stared at me, her head slightly bobbling.

"Tough audience," I said, as I stuffed the paper into my hand for another attempt. I "sneezed," and the tissue floated high above Sara's head. She shrieked with laughter.

I deployed this trick repeatedly throughout Sara's

toddlerhood. But if I didn't do it right, she'd look at me blankly, continue her screaming, or turn away and grab at a toy. Ever mindful that I needed new material, I continued to hone the comedy of the abrupt: having a stuffed animal suddenly burp, producing an object from nowhere, stumbling or falling.

Soon enough, physical humor gave way to blunt word play. Like George Carlin's seven words you can never say on network television, until she was close to six, Sara responded with various levels of laughter to any of the following terms, if timed correctly or placed in the right context: butt, booger, poop, fart (as a sound effect), pee-pee, and cack (as in a cat coughing up a hairball).

As she got closer to adolescence, word play became increasingly sophisticated, moving from knock-knock jokes, to puns, until finally, on a long road trip, we stumbled on a game we'd pull out anytime we were driving, and needed something to do.

"Beep, beep, beep, boop, beep, beep, boop. Ring, ring! Ring, ring!" I'd say.

"9.1.1., what's your emergency," answered Sara, in a nasal drawl she thought mimicked what a seen-it-all operator might sound like.

"Um, um, I need to go to the bathroom, and I don't know where the toilet is."

"Sir, this is 9.1.1. Do you have an emergency?" Sara drawled, in mock exasperation.

"Yes, I told you, I need to go, really, badly."

"Then go in the bushes!" She "slammed" the phone down angrily.

We'd go through several rounds of this joke, taking a turn as the caller – "I'm hungry, can you get me a snack;" "I'm feeling a little chilly, can you help me," "Uh, who am I calling?" – or the initially bored but helpful, and then angry, 911 operator. Each of us would try to get the biggest laugh possible, until finally, we'd go happily silent.

Handbook Tips: Games Daddy's Play
- ▶ There are plenty of comic ideas out there; just think like Jim Carey or the Three Stooges and you'll be fine. Keep in mind, though, that just as suddenly as the tricks work, at some point – when your baby becomes a toddler; as they emerge into adolescence – they won't anymore, and you'll need to change your material again.

- ▶ When Sara got older we invented the "hug or punch" game. It's easy to play: spot an actor, guy dressed up in a stuffed animal costume, or even relative and whisper "hug or punch?" The other player will choose based on what emotion the subject inspires. Caution: no actual punching! Though running up and hugging someone is generally encouraged.

Seize the Day

Sara had her first seizure when she was one. She was playing in "Dirty Park," a neighborhood playground given that nickname by our nanny, Gilda, because it featured a popular indoor area choked with large, well-loved, plastic toys that never seemed to be washed. As Sara convulsed, Gilda shouted to the other caretakers that something was wrong. A clutch of nannies – immigrants from Guatemala, El Salvador, and Mexico – gathered round to see how they could help. Someone called 911.

The paramedics arrived quickly, swept Sara up, and climbed into their ambulance. Gilda tried to follow.

"Are you related to this child?" asked the paramedic, as she blocked Gilda from getting into the vehicle.

"No, no, I'm her nanny," Gilda responded, her Guatemalan accent thickened with stress. "I'm responsible for her."

"Sorry ma'am, only relatives are allowed. You can follow her separately."

"But I don't have a car!" Gilda cried. But by that time the ambulance doors had shut, and the vehicle wheeled away.

I was working at home when my cell phone rang.

"Gilda just called me. Sara had a seizure. She's in an ambulance to the hospital. I'm in the car now," said Debbie.

"Which hospital?" I asked.

"The one on Geary Boulevard, where she was born. They're taking her to the emergency room."

I jumped into my car, and raced to the hospital, arriving at the emergency entrance just as the ambulance pulled up. A paramedic stepped out clutching Sara. Her clothes had been stripped off. She was naked, wrapped in a blanket, screaming.

"Is this your daughter?" she asked. I nodded.

"She was running a high temperature so we took her clothes off to cool her down," she said. Sara reached over and grabbed me, snuggling into my chest.

"She's seems to be okay now, though."

I rushed her into the hospital. Her screams turned to sobs, and then she relaxed into sleep on my chest. Debbie arrived 10 minutes later, though was delayed getting in as security demanded to see her identification.

Sara had experienced a febrile seizure, a convulsion triggered by rapidly rising fever. By the time she got to the hospital her temperature had mostly subsided. She exhibited no other health problems. We were told to take her home, make sure she drank liquids, and monitor her temperature.

Debbie and I were with Sara when she had her second seizure. She'd had a mild fever all day, which started to rise significantly as the sun set. As Sara's temperature swelled, Debbie called an advice-nurse, who told her to do what she could to get her fever down: take off her clothes, put her in tepid water. We tried everything, but Sara's fever stayed high, zooming past 104 Fahrenheit. And then she started to shake.

I've never experienced anything more frightening then seeing my baby daughter in full convulsions. I scooped her up; she felt like a steaming hot potato. Debbie called 911. A few moments later Sara stopped seizing, and went limp. I raced around the apartment holding her, thinking she might be dead.

The paramedics arrived. Debbie and I ran out of our apartment, Sara in my arms. Our downstairs neighbors, Joe and Sam, rousted by the ambulance's siren, were standing on the landing. Joe looked stricken. Sam, who was holding her new baby, Ella, in her arms, radiated maternal concern.

At the hospital the doctor told us that we needed to get fluids into Sara.

"We can put an IV in her," he said.

"She won't like that," I protested.

"I understand. We can take her and strap her down to get the needle into her arm. You don't even need to be in the room when we do the procedure."

"That's not going to happen," I said. "We're not leaving her alone, and we're not going to stick a needle into her."

"Well, you're not leaving here until she gets hydrated,"

replied the doctor. "You need to get enough liquid into her so that she pees."

The emergency room was packed with patients waiting to be seen, suffering from deep wounds, broken limbs, and other ailments. Since there weren't any treatment rooms available, we were directed to a couple of plastic chairs in the hallway. Over the next six hours – until 2 a.m. – we fed water to Sara from a needleless syringe. Each time she'd clamp her mouth shut. We'd beg and cajole her to take a few drops. We made a game out of it, flying the syringe like an airplane, or having it "walk" towards her month saying "water, water," a thirty girl lost in the desert.

New patients arrived; others were escorted into examination rooms. A man clutching his bloody stomach was wheeled in, and placed next to us, moaning. We continued to ply Sara with syringes of water. Periodically, Debbie or I would check her diaper, to see if she was wet.

"I felt something," Debbie finally said. "I think she peed!" She took off Sara's diaper; it was moist.

"I'll tell the nurse," I exclaimed, grabbing the soiled diaper and waving it in front of me like a trophy.

"It's wet! It's wet!" I said, as I hurried to the nurse who'd been monitoring us throughout the night.

She smiled. "I guess you can go home now."

We could have gone home within an hour of having arrived at the hospital, avoided camping out in the hallway as the nightly array of medical emergencies paraded by, if we'd just let the doctor put an IV in Sara. But we were unaccountably stubborn, especially given how freaked out we'd been about Sara's conditions just moments before. I'm glad we were; sometimes how care is delivered, and by whom, is as important as who is providing it.

Handbook Tips: Welcome to Disease Land!

▸ From the time they're born to early adolescence – if not longer – your kid will be visited by what will seem to be every single illness in a pediatrician's textbook: colds; flus; respiratory viruses; "slapped cheek;" hand, foot, and mouth disease; and a host of mysterious coughs, fevers, and rashes. If it's your first child you'll feel like you're trapped on a ship heaving through rough waters, with a foul, disease-ridden pack of sailors who like to breathe, spit, and vomit on you. Don't worry; this voyage will end. But, you may get many a bug along the way, including, in my case, walking pneumonia. Pull together a comprehensive medicine cabinet, including a few doses of Nyquil. You'll be needing those yourself.

▸ Doctors, teachers, counselors and other experts deserve great respect. But they only know so much, and nobody knows your child like you do. Sometimes being stubborn in the face of authority is exactly what you need to do.

▸ You can eat right, and exercise, but there's only one way to ward off communicable diseases: wash your hands! The filthiest place on earth isn't a men's room in Scotland; it's your local playground.

Daddy, What's That?

While shopping with two-year-old Sara at a local mall, I had to pee. Since I couldn't leave her by herself, I ushered her into the men's room, keeping her close by as I stood at the urinal next to another patron.

As I relieved myself Sara pointed towards my crotch and asked, "What's that Daddy?"

I glanced nervously at the man standing next to me. He seemed to be engaged in his own pursuits.

"That's called a penis," I said, in a voice that I hoped signaled the end of the conversation.

"Can I touch it?" Sara asked.

"Wait until we get home," I whispered back, though that wasn't exactly what I meant.

The man standing next to me zipped up and walked away. I did the same, washed my hands, and ushered Sara out

of the restroom.

Until Sara reached adolescence, I frequently had to troubleshoot bathroom visits when nature called her or me during an outing. Since I couldn't use the women's room, when she had to go I'd take her into a stall in the men's room. She mostly didn't mind. In fact, until Sara was in kindergarten she was convinced that she was actually a boy. More than once she asked Debbie or me "when's my penis going to grow?" For a couple of years my running joke with other new parents was that Sara could be whatever gender she wanted, but I wasn't going to pay for any operations.

Occasionally, Sara would refuse to go with me to the men's room – which tend to be stinky and sticky – forcing me to hold it until we got home. Once, after we'd dined at an IHOP in San Francisco, I badly needed to relieve myself. But no matter what I said I couldn't cajole Sara to come with me.

"I'll stay here," she insisted, as she used the complimentary crayons to color the paper placemat she'd been given.

I looked around the restaurant, which was sparsely populated with tourists, the elderly, and another family or two. The bathroom was behind the kitchen and down a hallway. Thoughts of baby snatchings popped into my head. Still, I really had to go.

"Wait right here. Don't go anywheres, no matter what," I said firmly.

"Okay," Sara smiled at me, looking like she'd just been giving the keys to a new sports car.

I ran to the bathroom, looking behind me to keep an eye on Sara as long as possible. I went in. The door automatically closed behind me. I pulled it back open and strode down the hallway far enough to see Sara. I could see the top of her head, her brownish-red hair looking like a messy nest, as she bent over her drawing. I went back into the men's room. The door closed behind me. I walked to the urinal and unzipped my pants.

"Shoot," I muttered to myself, nervously. I zipped my pants back up and strode out of the bathroom. Sara was still coloring. I went back to the bathroom, and finally finished my business.

After Sara turned five she began to embrace her girl identity, and completely balked at going into the men's room. The shark was jumped, so to speak, when, after a couple of years of doing so, she refused to get dressed in the boy's bathroom at the swimming class I took her to in Half Moon Bay. I couldn't blame her for not wanting to use that bathroom regardless of its gender designation. It was cramped, the toilet and shower stalls located hard on the small dressing area, the floors swampy with pool and shower water. At least I hoped that it was only water. Even I disliked it. Meanwhile, a peek at the girl's room indicated an ample-sized, carpeted dressing area well separated from the toilets.

The problem was, Sara refused to get dressed alone. She wanted me to help her. After we argued about it, I convinced myself that I was simply doing a father's duty, and went into the girl's room with her.

We put our belongings down on one of the benches, and Sara got into her bathing suit. A younger girl started to chat us up, asking where we got Sara's goggles, and what ribbon – the school awarded different colored stripes for various milestones – she was working on. All around us, though, girls older than Sara and their mothers were nervously eyeing me. The air began to feel heavy. I suddenly became aware that I was in, well, the girl's dressing room. I had infiltrated the "iron stall," going to a place no man is supposed to go. After Sara had finished, we gathered our stuff and hurried out.

As I watched Sara's swimming lesson, one of the facility's teenage clerks walked up to me.

"Mr. Moss, the manager wants to speak with you."

I followed the young woman to the reception area. As I approached a 30-something Asian-American woman who'd been talking to the manager, and who I recognized from the girl's room, gave me a sharp glance, and scuttled away.

"Mr. Moss," said the manager, as I stood at the counter, 'you can't go into the girl's room. You'll need to get your daughter dressed in the boy's bathroom."

"My daughter doesn't want to get dressed there anymore. She's a girl."

"I understand, but you can't go into the girl's room."

"But she can't get dressed without my help." I stared at the manager. She stared back at me. A co-worker, who'd been listening to the conversation, stepped up.

"Why don't you get dressed in the workout room? No one goes in there anyway."

And that's what happened. For the next several months,

before and after each Friday afternoon class, we'd go into the small, unused, workout room, and unpack Sara's clothes. She'd get dressed standing between the bench press and the stair master.

The space was ample, and private. But something about it felt awkward. Sara didn't like being segregated into this weighty no-man's land. It made her feel like she was different than her swim classmates. She wasn't a girl, getting dressed with her mom; or a boy with his dad. She was a daughter who changed her clothes with her daddy, something the swimming school, and the parents who took their children there, had signaled wasn't quite right, or at least not normal.

We didn't discuss it, but before long, though Sara was still two ribbons short of graduating, we stopped going to swimming lessons.

Handbook Tips: How to Avoid Changing Diapers

- ▸ You may not have noticed, since using a urinal can make them almost a hands-free experience, but public restrooms are nasty. You'll want to shield your loved ones from their worst offenses. Double wrap the toilet seat with those paper jobbies that are generally available. Remember, whatever your baby touches, eventually reaches her mouth, and then yours.

- ▸ Get a cool "diaper bag" – check out the bicycle messenger bags at your local sporting goods store – and make sure to always stow the key equipment: wipes, hand sanitizer, an extra diaper or two, and a fifth of your beverage of choice, which can serve as both an antiseptic and personal calmative in a pinch.

▸ There's going to be a lot of poop: up to five times a day, for more than two years. The best way to avoid having to deal with it is not being around when it's produced. Carefully study your baby's behavior to discover their tell. It could be a certain kind of grimace, or maybe a low grunting sound. Then, when the inevitable happens, don't panic. Just nonchalantly find a way to get out of there. A few possibilities: "Honey, I'm going out to get you some flowers, you deserve it!" Or, if that takes too long, "I just forgot, I left the car running!"

Falling Strollers

It's Sara's favorite story. She tells it at dinner parties and family gatherings: her near death experience when I allowed her unattended stroller to career down one of San Francisco's steepest hills. Even Debbie throws in details, and she wasn't there. I'll protest that, no, it didn't quite happen that way. But the particulars aren't important in the face of such cartoon-like daddy negligence. The tale is in the same mythic category as narrowly missing a toddler with a one-ton anvil, or leaving an opened bottle of Tylenol at baby level after a night out drinking (okay, I did that, but she didn't actually eat any).

Here's what happened. I walked three-year-old Sara down the two flights of stairs outside our San Francisco condominium. At street level – which tilts at something like a 45 degree angle – I strapped her into her stroller. We were set to go to Jackson Park, her favorite playground, a few blocks away.

Then I realized I didn't have my wallet with me. Crap. What if we needed to buy a snack?

I looked at her, happily playing in her stroller with two small stuffed animals. I looked up at the two flights of stairs. I made my decision.

Before I go on I need to tell you about the stroller. This wasn't one of those $500 turbo-charged models with built-in bottle warmer and fold-out diaper changing table; the kind our nanny, Gilda, used to say made her peers so nervous it'd be stolen that they'd spend more time watching the stroller than their charges. This was a $30 Costco umbrella stroller. No cup holder, no extra carrying case, no skid-proof wheel system, nothing.

I turned the stroller sideways against the hill. Despite what Debbie – remember, she wasn't there – or Sara – who at the time thought sand was edible – say, *I set the brakes*. I ran up the stairs, unlocked the door, grabbed my wallet, ran back down the stairs.

And she was gone.

There are a few moments in life when time stops. The universe seems to shudder and crack open, creating a new reality in which everything is different. Unless there are drugs or alcohol involved, this temporary suspension of time is never a good thing. It occurred to me when I took a hard tumble down a steep mountain slope skiing in Northern California. And it happened when I came down those stairs, and Sara wasn't where I'd left her. A set of feelings washed over me that I'd never previously experienced; a strange mix of stunned fear, sudden loss, and twisted resolve. My stomach churned; I felt

woozy.

Strangely, I looked up the hill. She wasn't there. I looked down the hill, into the street. I couldn't see where she went. I started down the slope. That's when I saw a small knot of Latino men running up the hill toward me, one of whom had my crying daughter cradled in his arms. They'd been gardening the front yard of a house a few doors down when she'd flown by in her stroller, before toppling over. I grabbed her from the man.

"Thank-you, thank-you," I said, as they placed her stroller and stuffed animals next to my house.

One side of Sara's face was scraped from her scalp to her chin, like a skinned knee. Other than that, and the shock of what'd happened, she was fine. I brought her upstairs, cleaned her up, and put her in front of her favorite video. Soon enough, she was back to her happy self. And then I had a thought, and the universe cracked open for a second time: how would I tell Debbie? I'll leave the specifics of that to another time. Perhaps it's enough to say that we're still married.

Handbook Tips: Caution, Contents under High Pressure
- ▸ You might feel compelled to purchase top-of-the-line strollers, high-chairs and the like. Spend as much as you want, if it makes you feel better. In the end it's the quality of the user more than the characteristics of the equipment that matters.

- ▸ There's an age-old question of whether, when taking off a bandage, to rip it off quickly or slowly. When it comes to telling your partner that you've just done something incredibly stupid with *their* baby, there's only one good approach: quick, clean, and comprehensive. Immediately followed by complete obeisance to whatever happens next. Think to yourself, "Yes, my liege!" But don't say it out loud.

▸ Your most embarrassing parenting moments will be retold repeatedly as epic stories for years to come by your child. No worries. Bide your time. Someday they'll get married, or have some kind of ceremony; that's when you get to give them a lengthy toast.

Rude Awakening

I was at the first day of a meditation retreat deep within New Mexico's mountains. The dozen participants assembled on the deck of the log cabin main lodge. We spent several hours getting to know one another, and learning the basics of mindfulness. As the sun dropped towards the horizon, each of us was assigned a pre-pitched tent, which were dispersed throughout the forest surrounding the lodge, none located less than a couple hundred yards from another. After a dinner of salad, rice, and chicken, and some casual conversation, we broke-up for the night, and made our way to our tents, flashlights in hand.

I unpacked my gear, placing a book and my flashlight on the wooden cart that served as a night stand, and got into my sleeping bag on top of a canvas cot. I was drifting towards sleep, when someone called out my name.

"Steven! Mr. Moss!" a man's voice urgently whispered. The tent flap flew open, and the center's night watchman thrust his head in. "You're wife just called. Your daughter is sick; she's at the hospital."

"What? What?" I said.

"Your wife," the watchman said more slowly. "She called the main office and said she took your daughter to the emergency room. She said she's okay, but she's in the hospital."

I immediately grabbed my things and started stuffing them into my duffel bag. "I need to get to the airport," I said. The man nodded.

Within minutes I was outside the tent, walking with the watchman, who was in his early 20s, towards the lodge, where the cars were parked, while simultaneously trying to call Debbie on my cellphone.

"We don't get cell service up here," the young man reminded me. "You'll have to wait until we get down the highway a few miles."

We walked in silence, the forest needles crunching beneath our feet. It was deep black, with an occasional star peeking through the overcast night. The watchman's large flashlight illuminated the trail and the trees crowded around it.

"You sure you want to leave?" he asked. "Your wife said your daughter was okay." He paused. "I mean, I'm happy to drive you."

"Thanks," I replied. "I need to go."

My heart was pounding from having been woken up by such distressing news, so far away from my wife and 18-month-old daughter. We got into the retreat center's truck, and started down the road. After several miles I tried my cell again; still no reception. I looked at my driver, and noticed the tattoos on his neck. Neither of us said anything, as I repeatedly punched the redial button. Finally, half-way down the mountain, I reached my wife in the emergency room.

"What's going on," I asked. "How's Sara?"

"She's okay," said Debbie. "She woke up after I put her to bed and couldn't breathe. She kept gasping for air. So I drove her to the hospital. She's okay now."

"What happened?"

"The doctors said she has some sort of respiratory virus. They gave her oxygen and some medicine." Debbie paused. "She's okay now," she repeated.

"Okay. I'm on my way to the airport. I'll catch the next flight home, though it may not be until morning. I'll get there as soon as I can"

"I don't think you need to do that," Debbie said. "When I called I was really worried, and thought you needed to know what was going on. But she's fine."

"I'm coming home," I said.

"Okay," Debbie sounded relieved. We hung up.

Two months after 9/11, Debbie, Sara, and I traveled to New York to attend a wedding. Though the ceremony was being held upstate from Manhattan, we were intensely curious about what had happened at the World Trade Towers, and wanted to see the destruction. Debbie questioned whether it was a good idea to bring a four-month-old near the site. But the federal government insisted that the air was safe.

Still in mid-hubris about being a new parent, and anxious to view the aftermath of the shocking events we'd seen on television, I didn't stop to consider that, no matter what the U.S. Environmental Protection Agency publicly stated, my daughter's new lungs would be especially sensitive to airborne particles, particularly the toxic kind that had to be floating around the site as a result of clean-up activities.

We checked into our hotel, and took a taxicab to as close to where the World Trade Towers once stood as we could. We slowly strollered Sara around the massive craters, peeking through what was left of the towers, gapping at the astonishing destruction. Occasionally a passerby would glance at our baby and give us a hard look, but, swept away by disaster-sized curiosity, I hardly noticed.

A little more than a year after our New York visit I got the call that woke me from my meditation tent, and brought me home to my family. For the following year Sara struggled with a respiratory problem, the origin and nature of which our doctors couldn't define. Debbie or I would regularly have to strap a mask over Sara's mouth and nose and dose her with vaporized medicine. We were deeply rattled, concerned about our daughter's health and worried that, without a proper diagnosis, we'd never be able to solve her problem. And in the wake of my late-night New Mexico experience I'd tense every time Debbie called, afraid that she was going to report bad news about Sara.

I don't know if our visit to the 9/11 site is what caused Sara's respiratory problems. But it was stupid for us to bring our baby daughter anywhere near what by all accounts was a smoldering, toxic crater. And there's no lost irony that I was at a meditation retreat, about to go to sleep, when I received a wake-up call.

Handbook Tips: Attention!

▸ I don't know about you, but I tend to get trapped in my immediate past, and tripped up by visions of my lofty future. It took me several years after I got married to stop flirting with other women, not because I didn't love my wife; it was just a well-worn habit. I maintained my youthful wanderlust through most of Sara's young life, dragging her and Debbie to India when she was a toddler and to Africa before she was five. It's important to know when one life phase has ended – you were single; now you're married – and another has begun. You gotta dress for the right occasion.

▸ There's no need to fool ourselves, being a father can sometimes be a big fat drag. But, mostly, it's a lot of fun. Remember the latter when you're in the middle of the former.

Busy Dad

"Lie down, Poppy," three-year-old Sara instructed me. "Pretend you're deaded."

I lay on my back on the rug and stuck my tongue out, in her required pose. Sara knelt next to me, inspecting each of my body parts. Sometimes she'd have a toy animal crawl over my leg or chest, like it was climbing a mountain.

"Don't move!" she ordered, when I flexed an ankle. "Stay still!"

Sara loved this game. It wasn't playing doctor, as she didn't use her plastic medical instruments, and never diagnosed any shots or pills. But during it she was able to keep me immobilized, under her control. I wasn't allowed to check my smartphone for email. If the telephone rang, I couldn't answer it. I just had to lie, completely still and do nothing.

After Sara was born, I committed to caring for her at

least one day during the work week – sometimes managing two – and tried to be home by mid-afternoon daily. It was a promise I wanted to make, to spend time with my baby daughter, with whom I'd fallen deeply in love. But like many working parents, when I was with Sara my mind was often elsewhere, particularly in her first several months. As soon as she seemed to be occupied by something – an interactive mobile, chewable rattles – I'd rush over to my computer to squeeze in some work. Inevitably, within minutes – sometimes seconds – Sara would get bored with her activity – or hungry or messy – and start crying. I'd curse under my breath, run back over to her, take care of her needs, and hurry back to the computer.

It was no way to live. The stop-start process kept my irritability at a low simmer, which sometimes boiled over as a result of sleeplessness. But I kept at it, compulsively trying to get work done in between tending Sara, despite her regular shock treatments of crying right when I was in the middle of crafting an "essential" message to a client or friend. I was caught between the gratification of getting tasks done, and the pain of being interrupted by my daughter, all the while feeling guilty that I wasn't lavishing my full attention on her.

Babies might not know much, but they're not stupid. It didn't take long for Sara to pick up on my inattentiveness, and invent a game to (temporarily) overcome it. And I enjoyed it, at least for a while. There was something delicious about letting my toddler stop me from doing anything. Over time, by cleverly reminding me to just be still, she helped me break my work-obsessed-habits. To be, to use a perhaps overused word, "present."

At least most of the time. I still check email, or try to get work done, when Sara is busy playing or reading while in my care. But when she calls me on it I quickly put the phone down, or save the message, and turn my full attention to her. I don't even think about cursing.

Handbook Tips: Distracting Your Child

▸ *Can stay-at-home professional work and taking care of your child co-exist?* The short answer is, no, not unless you're willing to rely on that one-eyed monster, the television set (or, for modern fathers, the iPad). Assume that for our purposes that you're a responsible dad; then what do you do? Here's a couple of ideas:

(1) *Pretend you're parallel playing.* Put your child in front of their favorite toys; place yourself in front of one of yours, mostly likely a computer or smartphone. As you "work" act all floppy and giggly, as if you're enjoying yourself, taking a break every five to 10 minutes to gurgle loudly, or grab a desk object, though make sure it's nothing you actually need. Seeing you having such a good time, your baby will do the same! Caution: remember to hit the mute button when you're on a conference call.

(2) *Don't do the dishes, take a shower, or shave, or, if you have to, do them all at once in the shower.* By cutting out these extraneous activities you'll

buy yourself some time that you can dedicate to work. If your partner complains about the pile of plates in the sink, ask her if she cleans the kitchen in *her* office. Your love life might suffer, but, then again, what love life?

▶ *If you work at an office, take your baby with you.* Make sure she's dressed in her cutest outfit, and is clutching her most beloved stuffy. Sit her on your lap at your desk, and coo loudly. Before too long you should be able to attract a 20-something woman who'll whisk the little one off to the break room, giving you a chance to get some real work done.

Sleep is a Delicate Thing

"*Reaux*, Sham, *Beaux*, sudden death!" Debbie announced, invoking our last ditch method of determining which one of us would have to do whatever unpleasant task was at hand.

"Mommy! Daddy!" Sara screamed from her bedroom. Both of us had already tucked her in multiple times. On each occasion, not long after we sat back down to finish dinner, she'd loudly demanded that we come back to her bedside. Glancing at my almost cold bowl of homemade macaroni and cheese, I raised my fist in preparation for battle with Debbie to decide which of us would return to Sara's room.

Sleep is a foreign country Sara would rather not visit. As soon as she could make an understandable sound she insisted that Debbie or I crawl onto the mattress next to her, and stay there until she closed her eyes. Every night my wife or I would either fall asleep in her bed well before 8:30 p.m., or lie with her for more than an hour before slowly extracting ourselves from her tight grip.

Getting out of Sara's bed was like defusing a bomb. She tended towards a defensive sleeping posture, wrapping a slender arm around my neck, in a kind of modified choke-hold; and/or throwing one of her legs over my waist. I needed to quietly and carefully shift her appendages off from wherever they were draped on my body. I usually deployed one of her large stuffed animals to switch out her neck hold, letting her grip that instead. To remove her leg was more difficult, usually requiring that she be in deep sleep.

Once her initial sleep traps had been eliminated, I'd slowly scoot down the mattress, away from her body, like crawling under barbed wire. I'd then slide down the edge of her chest bed, feet stretched out to find a clear space on the floor. The next stage was critical: avoiding stepping on the toys scattered around her room, being especially careful not to disturb an object that, when squished, would squeak, squeal, or honk, waking her up, and triggering a repeat of the entire excruciating process. This happened more than once, causing me to whisper angry curses at whoever gave her the stuffed dog that barked when squeezed, or the electronic toy that played a merry tune when jostled.

The exception to Sara's war against sleep occurred during an eight week trip to Southern India when she was three years old. The place's intensity was overwhelming, filled with

swirling, colorful saris, the smell of dirt mixed with sewage, spices, and exhaust, and the cacophony of shouting vendors, rumbling cars and motorcycles, joined by the occasional passage of a clambering religious or political mini-parade. Going unconscious was Sara's defense. As soon as we got into an auto-rickshaw – a three-wheel vehicle with a sheet metal cabin bolted over a two-person bench, pulled by a high-pitched four-cycle engine – Sara would fall asleep against my chest. Minutes after the start of a Kathakali dance recital, which featured masked and costumed performers, drumming and high-pitched singing, she crawled onto my lap, turned away from the stage, and slept.

Back in San Francisco, Debbie and I loathed Sara's insistence on bedtime companionship, and bitterly fought over whose turn it was to put her to sleep. But we were also sympathetic – it made sense to us that she'd want to snuggle with someone else, something we ourselves enjoyed – and hopeful that her fitful sleep habits would end soon.

"She's not going to want to sleep with us when she's a teenager," Debbie desperately joked, her voice tilting towards a question mark at the end.

We both knew that we'd caused the problem, by mishandling Sara's sleep habits early on. This shouldn't have been allowed to fester so long. Still, our night time lives were being obliterated. A few weeks after we returned from India we decided to "Ferber" Sara. The Ferber Method supposedly trains children to "self-soothe" by steadily increasing their tolerance for being left alone. We'd tuck Sara in, fend off her protests, slink out the door, and wait in the kitchen while she cried. The initial five minutes of sobbing turned into 10, and then 20. Days passed, but the method wasn't working, or we weren't allowing it to. If we didn't go comfort her, Sara would get out of her bed and find us, demand a new tucking-in, and repeat the cycle. Inevitably, after an hour of back-and-forth, with no sign that Sara would relent, one of us – usually me – would capitulate, and crawl into bed with her.

Finally, one night, we decided to stand our ground.

"Neither of us is giving in this time," Debbie said firmly. We read to Sara, carefully smoothed the blankets over her, slipped her favorite stuffy, Koda, into her arms, kissed her goodnight, and told her that no one was going to sleep with her tonight or in the future.

"No!" Sara, shouted, "Sleep with me!"

We walked out of her room, and gently shut the door. Sara cried. We stayed where we were, sitting on the sofa in the living room. Sara got out of bed, and begged us to come tuck her in. We told her to go back to bed. She'd return to her room, only to cycle back out 20 minutes later. Days went by; the battle went on for hours every night. Still, Debbie and I held firm.

A week and a half into the Ferber skirmishes, Sara got out of bed for the second time that night. She stood in her too big racecar pajamas – hand-me-downs from her cousin, Asa – clutching Koda, one hand rubbing an eye.

"Go back to bed," I said, firmly.

"Mommy, daddy, I need to tell you something," Sara said.

"Okay," Debbie said. "What?"

"It hurts my feelings when you walk away from me at bedtime, and it makes me feel bad when you tell me to go back to bed all of the time," Sara sniffled. "I'm just a child."

Surprised by the crack of a new maturity in Sara's voice, neither of us knew whether to smile at her truthful expression of her feelings, or frown in response to this new, emotionally savvy tactic. But we both knew that Ferbering was finished.

"Come on, Sweetie, I'll put you to bed," said Debbie.

An hour or so later my wife came out of Sara's room, yawning. "She's asleep," she said.

"What do we do now?" I asked.

"I don't know," said Debbie. "We may not have taught her to put herself to sleep, but I guess we did teach her to communicate her feelings. That's something."

Handbook Tips: Sleepy or Weepy

▸ You have a choice. You can be firm about bed time, tucking in your kids like clockwork, never letting them get up after they've been handed their stuffy or other favorite sleep object, and been fully blanketed. Or, you can be all loosey-goosey, and let things slip-slide away. Create a cozy "family" bed, fetch them water on demand, allow them to get up and go to the bathroom. And never have sex with your partner at home again without wondering whether someone will come padding in during the act. Your call.

▸ Lots of kids don't like to sleep alone; who can blame them? My sister, Marissa, solved this problem by having two of her three boys sleep together until they were in kindergarten, an arrangement that worked well for all involved. Another option: get a dog or cat, and have the critter sleep with your child. Animals can be costly, and leave pesky hair and dirt around, but it's all worth it if it gets your kid to stay in bed at night.

▶ Some things go in phases, others might last a good long time. Nearly a decade after our Ferber wars Sara still fights going to sleep. She follows a nightly battle plan that starts with playing in bed, shifts to reading in bed, and typically ends with her insisting I tell her a story. Most nights she appears at least once after she's been tucked-in, marches to wherever we are, and announces, "I have a question," followed by a mostly irrelevant query about the next day's activities, or something that happened at school. I'll escort her back to bed, fold the covers over her, and kiss her, once again, good night.

Bad Cook

I've never been a good cook. In college I subsisted on Top Ramen and canned chili. As a young man, if I invited a woman over for dinner I'd either buy prepared food or follow one of a handful of recipes taken from a tattered copy of the *Joy of Cooking* I'd pilfered from my grandmother: spaghetti, baked fish, steak, or stir fry.

When I was growing up no one expected men to cook. The best my father could do was a serving of cottage cheese mixed with jelly, or peanut butter sandwiches, which he oddly heated in the oven before serving.

In the kitchen I'm sloppy, impatient, and ill-trained. I tend to hack at things as opposed to cut them, and glop condiments and other items on rather than spread them evenly. Once, while dining with a few friends, one of them took the bagel on which I was messily applying cream cheese out of my hand, carefully covered it with the cheese, and handed it back to me.

"It needs to be fully spread, evenly around all the edges," he said, without cracking a smile. "Otherwise, it's not good."

"Thanks," I mumbled, simultaneously irritated and grateful. I have to admit, it did taste better.

Debbie, however, is an excellent cook, making delicious food with great care and skill. Give her three ingredients and a rack of spices, and she'll return with a four star, five course meal. Until we had Sara we relied on her abilities for sustenance, if we weren't eating out. When Sara was first born Debbie breastfed her, though since she wouldn't "latch-on" that required nearly a year of unpleasant pumping, a difficult kind of cooking.

I needed to step up my culinary skills when Sara started to eat solid foods. She didn't much like processed baby food, nor did we. Since she was so small, to fatten her up our pediatrician suggested avocado, a nutrient-rich, easy to eat, fruit. Our nanny, Gilda, came up with a simple recipe, which Debbie quickly perfected into an "avocado sandwich:" smooshed avocado mixed with a bit of salt, wrapped into triangular flour tortilla tubes. Sara loved them, eating a sandwich two, sometimes three, times a day. Which meant when I was taking care of her I had to make it.

Recall that the concoction had three ingredients: avocado, salt, and flour tortilla. But I couldn't get it right. Even after Gilda gifted us with a wooden implement from Guatemala that she said would help smoosh the avocado evenly and keep it from going brown prematurely, my mush would end up to too chunky, or with not enough salt. Or I'd fold the tortilla tubes incorrectly, leaving flour flaps and holes where Debbie created a perfect cone. Each time I prepared Sara's favorite meal, she'd reject it, sending back the food like a disgruntled diner at an upscale restaurant.

I carefully watched Debbie as she made the dish. Really, how hard could this be? It took several attempts, but finally I got it right. It was perfect, exactly how Debbie prepared it. I brought a plate of sandwiches to Sara. She took one bite, and waved it away.

"But, what's wrong with it," I exclaimed.

"No lemon!" said, Sara, who hadn't yet turned four.

"Mommy doesn't put lemon in it," I protested.

"Yes she does!" she insisted.

The real problem was that I'd trained Sara to know that I wasn't a good cook. It no longer mattered how well I executed an avocado sandwich. I'd become the opposite of an advertising tagline from my childhood – "With a name like Smucker's, it has to be good" – turning myself into, "If it's made by Steven, it can't be edible."

I knew that with practice I could make a sandwich that would taste and look exactly the same as Debbie's. And I did. But there was only one way to overcome my branding problem: lie. The next time Sara asked for her preferred meal I called out loudly,

"Debbie, will you make Sara an avocado sandwich?"

Then, while Sara busied herself with her toys, I hurried

into the kitchen and made the thing myself. As I placed it on the table I shouted, as if I was on a long-distance telephone call from yesteryear, "Here you go; Mommy made it."

Sara loved the sandwich.

I employed this tactic for several weeks. Until one day, after Sara had tucked away half her meal, I announced, "You know, I made that sandwich."

"You did," she said, looking at her mom.

"Yep," I replied, proudly.

"It's pretty good," she munched.

From then on I was allowed to make Sara her avocado sandwiches. I thought I'd jumped to the next level as a household cook. Until Sara's tastes shifted, and she started to reject three ingredient sandwiches in favor of a Debbie-developed vegetarian "hamburger:" plain bun, tomatoes, mayonnaise, and mustard. It had just four components. But it took me weeks to master it.

Handbook Tip: Using Your Baby as a Human Shield

▸ Bored, tired, or irritated by an event or group of friends or relatives? No problem, as long as you have your child with you. Just blame them for having to suddenly leave any unpleasant situation, temporarily or forever. Even if your child isn't immediately present, they exist somewhere in the world: you may need to call them to check-in, or perhaps your babysitter's time is up. A huge benefit of fatherhood is having this built-in, no-questions-asked, excuse to disappear. Take full advantage of it.

▸ Babies and small children also come in handy at public gatherings. Sara frequently accompanied me to anti-war, pro-environmental rallies in her early years. Wearing an adorable ladybug-patterned red beanie, she attracted a Japanese newscaster during a rally against the first Gulf War, who interviewed me while her cameraman trained his equipment on Sara. She was in my arms multiple times when I spoke at community meetings to close down power plants. And babies and small children can be useful to get on planes early, or to secure a front row seat at a crowded venue. Don't be shy, lead with you kid!

Ping Pong Balls from Heaven

There's nothing my father likes better than getting something for nothing. During Southern California's 1970s-era real estate boom almost every weekend he'd make a round of the local savings and loans, caging free cookies and coffee. He has a constant stash of hundreds of pens, key chains, and hard-to-define objects — hand-held squishy toys, or decorative desk objects — picked up at conferences or grand openings. If there's a going out of business sale he'll want to go, even if what's being offered isn't anything he needs.

When I was 12, living in Palos Verdes, he gathered my mom, three sisters and me and told us that we were going to a promotion at a new shopping mall. A helicopter was going to fly over the mall's parking lot and drop hundreds, maybe thousands, of ping pong balls on the crowd below. Printed on each ball would be a discount coupon for clothes, maybe, or a free cola at the food court. Most importantly, though, a rare number of balls would deliver something finer: a brand new car, or all-you-could-eat at Bob's Big Boy.

After my dad finished explaining the possibilities, as well as the challenges, my mom decided she didn't want go. I, however, was eager for prizes. I equipped myself with a baseball mitt; my father took the long-handled net from our goldfish pond. My sisters brought nothing. We jumped into the family's Ford Comet station wagon, and made our way to whatever suburb the mall had recently been planted in. Maybe it was in Torrance, or Pasadena. I don't remember, and, in Southern California, it doesn't really matter.

We were surprised by the size of the crowd. The parking lot was jammed with people. Some had nets; not the puny kind that my father held, but huge web-type things that might have been used to haul in giant sea turtles, or catch pterodactyls. Others held something more rudimentary, like a cardboard box, or blanket. I milled among the assembled crowd, my nose about the height of an average armpit, thinking, "no way are we catching any balls," but also mustering all of the determination and competitiveness I could. I didn't want to walk away empty-handed.

Scanning the parking lot stuffed with people gripping nets, blankets, boxes, and plastic containers, the mall people must have been at least a little concerned. The crowd wasn't exactly unruly, but, hey, there was free stuff at stake. And there were a lot of us, probably more than expected, strangers all jockeying for position, though not knowing what a good position would be. Family knots and small groups of men and women were murmuring together, occasionally scanning the cloudless skies.

Soon enough, the whir of a helicopter could be heard nearby. All heads turned upwards to identify the prey, shifting to some other, perhaps better, location. The helicopter hovered for a few moments, surveyeing the crowd. I've got to think somebody up there said, "You know, maybe this isn't such a good idea after all." But it was too late for that. And from above, the copter released its load.

For what seemed like a long time, the white specks stayed where they were, high in the air, suspended. Then, they rained down. People grabbed. People yelled. Balls fell into nets and popped back out. A half-dozen large men leapt for the same ball at once, and struggled for possession.

I quickly discovered that I was too short to snag a ball while it was airborne. I scuttled around people's knees, searching for fallen prizes. I snatched a ping pong ball as it squirted along the ground, and held it fiercely in my hand.

Soon, the last of the balls had been captured. It was like a giant wind had passed through. People struggled back to their families and friends. I found my father and sisters, ball-less all. My dad claimed a ball had directly hit his net, and bounced back out. I believed him, but the ball I held in my hand was real. I held it out to examine the tattoo plastered on its plastic. I'd won 50 cents at one of the mall's shoe stores. The lady at the counter didn't smile as she handed me the shiny half-dollar coin.

My dad and my sisters sat silently in the car, exhausted from the struggle, and disappointed that they'd won nothing.

In the back seat, I clutched my 50 cent piece tightly in my fist. I knew it wouldn't last long.

Sara has never had to wait for a ping pong ball to drop out of the sky to get what she wants. Almost everything she desires – except a second dog, younger sibling, or the latest iPhone – she gets from Debbie or me. Recently, a wealthy friend offered to fly Debbie and Sara on a chartered plane to her house in Hawaii. At dinner, Debbie relayed the offer to Sara.

"So, do you want to go" Debbie asked.

"I'll think about it," Sara said, flatly.

Debbie and I looked at one another.

"Um," I said, "Did you hear what you're mom said? Vacation in Hawaii? Private plane?"

Such largess would have been unimaginable in my household growing up – something that would only happen on television – and remarkable even in Debbie's childhood home, which included the occasional exotic vacation and housekeepers, but not chartered jets to enchanted islands.

"Yeah, I heard," said Sara, as she chewed on a piece of avocado sushi. "I said I'll think about it."

I'm not sure what provides a better foundation for adulthood, growing up with scarcity, or being raised with plenty. I suppose, if I had a choice, I'd choose abundance. We'll see how that works out.

Handbook Tips: Dream a Little Dream
- ▸ Up until she turned 10 Sara loved to study the latest toy

catalogue and circle what she liked, typically marking many pages. She didn't seem to mind that we never bought her any of the items. At Halloween she wouldn't stop trick or treating until her extra-large bag was filled with sugary tidbits, though there's never been a year in which she's eaten even a quarter of the proceeds. No need to promise your kid the moon, but if you give them half of what they say they want that'll be plenty.

▶ There's nothing better than a lemonade stand to give your child a chance to earn some spare change. The entire enterprise has iconic status – particularly in a low-kid population city like San Francisco – from the misspelled and crooked sign, to the compostable Dixie cups into which the lemon-dusted beverage is dispensed. On our corner, on a sunny day, Sara and a friend or two can earn upwards of $150 over a four hour period; better than minimum wage at a fast food restaurant. Childhood only comes around once; make sure your kid has a chance to cash in on their cuteness.

Crosses to Bear

When Sara was five I gave her a Christian cross. Not on purpose; we're Jewish. It came as a prize from a gumball machine. She'd put her quarter in, spun the dial, popped open the small plastic bubble, and put the cross around her neck before I even noticed.

"What's this," she asked, looking down at her chest.

"A cross," I said, and left it at that. Like most of her cheap toys, I knew it'd be forgotten the next day.

I examined the gumball machine. There was no indication that it sold religious objects, or that it was sponsored by a church. It might actually be fun to take your chances on a grab bag of spiritually-oriented items – a tiny prayer rug; a *driedel*; or maybe a plastic bubble containing nothing for the Buddhists. But to pay two-bits in the expectation that your kid will get a plastic ring, or Scooby-Doo sticker, and receive

Christianity's primary object didn't sit right with me.

We're surrounded by religious, commercial, and social messages. San Francisco's cityscape features St. Mary's cross, City Hall's dome, and the Transamerica Pyramid. But increasingly we're being proselytized from unexpected sources. Products are strategically placed in movies and television shows. Politicians pay to be included in purported news stories. Proto-hipsters are given free sneakers. Internet searches come with complimentary, especially tailored to you, pop-up advertisements.

Recently, Debbie did a Google search for a recipe. First in line in the results were instructions from her father's foster mother, which triggered the increasingly familiar emotional response: excitement – someone I know or am related to came up in my Internet search! –suspicion – How is that possible? Out of thousands of recipes, why is hers listed first? – paranoia – Google is tracking my every move, knows I'm related to her, and that's why she came up first. What else do they know about me? – followed by attention span expiration; hey, that flash site is having a sale on mani-pedis!

Though the ability to hype may have reached hyper-speed, it isn't a new phenomenon. As Christian legend has it, the devil wears many faces. Our job is to recognize him whatever his disguise. The only difference between the current chaotic period – in which beliefs quickly evolve into facts – and what our ancestors experienced 500 years ago, may be the volume of information to sift through.

In the end, we're the ones who name the devil. We give things their meaning, whether it be instilling power in a given object or making sense of a politician's pitch. And maybe, in our message-laden world, that's how we should approach most communication. The next time something unexpected pops out of life's gumball machine I'll take it at face value. After all, in the presence of complete ignorance about Christianity, a cross is just a piece of jewelry.

At least until we got home, when, after Sara had taken the cross off and put it on her dresser, Debbie discretely disposed of it. By then Sara had already forgotten about it, which may be the most apt response to superficially-delivered messages' staying power. They only last as long as we want them to.

Handbook Tips: Religion
- Until your kid reaches early-adolescence, you're God, able to direct them to worship pretty much anything: the Easter Bunny, baseball, nature, SpongeBob. This power will dissipate over time, with childhood beliefs in a host of magical creatures – Santa Claus, the Tooth Fairy, your infallibility – dropping off like so many baby teeth. Yet even after your kid has drifted off towards video games or shopping, a residue of faith will be left behind from which their future values will grow. What remains is partially determined by you: the charity you engage in as they grow up, the community you belong to, the religious services you attend. In the end, your children are most likely going to choose some kind of religion. Which one is largely up to you.

- Even if you're anti-religion, your kid will need an

identity or activity to fall back on when life gets tough. Hiking or camping is good, as is learning how to play a musical instrument. Try to avoid modeling binge eating or shopping, though excessive cleaning and organizing can have its upsides. Debbie finds solace in organizing things into carefully marked boxes: shoes, medicines, office supplies, even smaller boxes. A bit obsessive, perhaps, but it can come in handy when trying to locate a rarely used object.

Kiss Therapy

We were driving a modest distance, Debbie at the wheel, when four-year-old Sara started to fuss, over what I don't remember, and it doesn't really matter. The fuss escalated into a full-on tantrum, with screaming and kicking.

"If you don't stop that right now I'm going to pull this car over," Debbie sternly announced, invoking a parental warning that was included in Ford's original Model T's owner manual.

Sara did not stop. Debbie abruptly wheeled the vehicle to the curb, parked it on the shoulder, jumped-out the driver's side door, opened the passenger door, grabbed Sara, and enveloped her in a huge hug.

"You look like you need some loving," she said.

Sara's screams diminished to sobs, sniffles, and, then, quiet.

I don't know how Debbie came up with this brilliant approach, which turned mid-century last child-rearing norms upside down. She was raised by divorced parents, her mother intermittently absent and smothering, her father a practitioner of benign neglect. As for me, my mom was also a follower of the benign neglect parenting model, while my dad was a hair-trigger screamer, which left me with a deep aversion to conflict, which continues to linger.

"I just thought why not replace anger with love. I mean, she is my daughter," Debbie later explained to me.

While not always successful, we've tried to adopt the "love not anger" approach as a family habit. Not long after Sara's tantrum Debbie and I got into a furious argument; again I can't recall over what. In the middle of it, after Debbie had just finished making a triumphantly sarcastic retort to whatever I'd previously irritatingly asserted, I walked over to her, grabbed her, and kissed her.

"What are you doing," she asked, still half-livid.

"You can't be angry at someone when they're kissing you," I responded.

Since then we've frequently practiced "kiss therapy." It doesn't always work, and sometimes both of us are too stubborn – or mad – to execute it. But it's repeatedly demonstrated its ability to overpower other, more traditional, couple's fight tactics, including the silent treatment, mocking, and caustic comments. A well-intentioned kiss can muffle a thousand angry words.

A while ago, Sara brought home a report card that indicated some serious slippage in a few key areas.

"What's going on," I asked her, while the three of us were finishing dinner around our kitchen table.

"I don't want to talk about it," she insisted, her voice rising.

"Well, you don't have to talk about it now, but you do before you watch television again," I said. Which prompted an escalating outburst from Sara, pre-pubescent-style: stomping, leaving the room, coming back, yelling.

"It's none of your business!" she shouted at me, as she sat back down at the table.

Debbie got up from her chair, knelt-down, and gave Sara a tight hug.

"Go away!" she shouted half-heartedly, struggling against the embrace.

"I'm not going away," Debbie responded, "I'll never go away."

Debbie ushered Sara out of the kitchen, her arm across our daughter's hunched shoulders, into Sara's bedroom. I followed, and listened by the door, but their voices were muffled, which I took as a good sign. With Debbie's help, Sara must have calmed herself.

Debbie emerged some time later, and let me know that they'd discussed her report card; we'd debrief later. Whatever Sara's problem, it just needed some loving to solve it.

Never Mind that Giraffe

"Look, Sara, look!" whispered Debbie, as she stared up at a giraffe, not 10 feet from where she stood.

We were just outside Niamey, the capital of Niger, at a game preserve that held the last clutch of giraffes in all of West Africa. We seemed to be in the middle of the herd, surrounded by the magical creatures. We'd parked our vehicle, and wandered less than a mile into a marsh accompanied by our driver and a guide. Along the way we'd passed termite mounds larger than Sara, and small pools of water thick with insects and tadpoles. One of which five-year-old Sara was examining when Debbie called her name.

"Look," I repeated to Sara, "Giraffes!"

Sara ignored us, instead squatting down to take a closer look at the tadpoles. As a giraffe ambled behind us in its prehistoric lope, followed by her calf, Sara wandered a few steps

to a termite mound, which she kicked.

"What's this, Da Da?" she asked.

"A termite hill. Termites live in it. But look at the giraffes," I pleaded, gesturing towards the long-necked spotted creatures around us.

Sara pretended not to hear me. For the rest of our time in the preserve she kept her head down, searching the ground, streamlets, and ponds for insects, amphibians, and flowers. If you asked her today whether she saw any giraffes when we were in Niger, she'd say, "No." And I'm afraid she'd be right.

We'd had a similar experience with Sara the year before, when we were on a safari in Tanzania. We'd driven into the Ngorongoro Crater in a safari car with a pop-up roof, past herds of wildebeest, zebra, and eland, and had stopped to admire a small knot of gazelles, Debbie and I leaning over the top of the vehicle to get a better view. As we'd driven through the crater, four-year-old Sara had rotated between standing on a seat next to us to eye the animals – she especially liked the zebras – and dropping to the floor of our modified Land Cruiser to play with a set of plastic animals she'd brought with her.

Out on the savanna, most of the gazelles bounded away, leaving one straggler behind. I could almost hear the ominous nature film narrator's voice, intoning the danger confronting an animal that's been separated from its herd. Our driver, Debbie, and I scanned the tall grasses in front of us, looking for more animals.

"Whoa," I whispered. "Look over there!" I gestured

towards a clump of brush, through which a large orange-spotted cat seemed to be crawling on its belly in the direction of the gazelle.

Our guide pointed his binoculars in the direction I'd indicated. 'It's a cheetah!" he said, a ting of excitement in his voice. "It's stalking that gazelle!"

We looked back and forth from the cheetah to the gazelle, which bounded a few yards, froze for a moment, and then bounded again, in no particular direction.

"Sara, come look," Debbie whispered.

"Yeah, come on, come on!" I urged.

Sara didn't budge, continuing to play with her toys.

"It's okay," whispered our guide, "this could take several hours."

We settled into our watchful standing positions, mindful that we could be there awhile, and refocused on the unfolding drama. The cheetah didn't take its eyes off the gazelle, stealthy crawling forward when the herbivore was busy chewing grass. Several minutes passed.

"Sara, you should really look at this," I said, turning towards her. "It's a cheetah stalking a gazelle."

She stayed on the floor, playing with her toys. I looked back at the cheetah, which abruptly launched itself into a run. The gazelle seemed to sense the attack, and started rapidly bounding in a zig-zag pattern. But it was too late. Within seconds the cheetah was on top of it, biting its neck. A few moments later it was dragging the now dead gazelle away in its jaws.

"Wow," Debbie exclaimed, "Did you see that?"

I nodded, smiling.

A little while later, we rolled back to a rest area, and got out of the Land Cruiser.

"Hey," exclaimed Sara, "what's this?" She pointed at a large brown mound a few yards from where we'd parked.

"That's elephant poop," our guide laughed.

"Cool!" Sara shouted. "Mommy, take my picture!"

Sara posed next to the lump of dung. It's what she remembers most from our safari.

Handbook Tips: Travel

Setting aside your own desire to visit exotic places, until your kid is a certain age traveling to the local park is way more attractive to them than going to Paris or Patagonia. Here's a quick guide to preferred child charters:

- ▸ *Up to two-years old*: Local playgrounds and occasional visits to relatives is all they need. Long car trips may lull them to sleep – good – but windy roads can make them vomit – bad – and be mindful of places to stop to change diapers, and buy key supplies.

- ▸ *Two to five years old*: Places with pools, beaches, and amusement parks are all good. Careful of losing them in crowds!

- ▸ *Five to eight years old*: Hands-on museums, camping, and skiing are fun and, can be educational. Make them carry as much of their own equipment as possible.

▸ *Eight and up*: Hit the road! Bring various distractions – play 20 questions, license plate alphabet, I spy – and try to save the games, videos, and electronics for when they're needed most. There's nothing like travel to bring families together, and to irritate the $%#! out of them.

Candy Man

An old joke, repeated in Woody Allen's *Annie Hall*, neatly sums up the food situation in my childhood home. Two elderly women are eating at a Catskill mountain resort.

"Boy," one of them says, "The food at this place is really terrible."

"Yeah, I know; and such small portions!" responds the other.

Perhaps it was her Depression-era upbringing, or how she was treated by her mother, but my mom was an inattentive tightwad when it came to the food she doled-out to my three sisters and me. She'd serve lumpy powdered milk in white Melmac cups. If we didn't completely finish our portion, the partially filled cup would go into the refrigerator, often smudged with fingerprints or food crumbs lingering around it, to be served again, and again, until we drank it or, more often, found a clandestine way of disposing of it. In the face of our stubborn resistance to this protocol, eventually my mom stopped serving us milk altogether.

Small portions of inexpensive snacks were available twice a day – afterschool, and as a dessert after dinner – on a schedule specified to the minute, though on weekends our dad might escort us to a bank opening, where we'd scarf down free goodies. Every night my sisters and I would line up at the kitchen threshold, eyeing the plastic plate of snacks sitting on a counter, as the seconds ticked towards the appointed time, anxious to be the first to snatch up a half dollar-sized cookie purchased from the day-old bakery outlet – or gathered for free by my dad at a local savings and loan – a piece of sliced apple or a wedge of orange.

My mom's food practices didn't seem to have any disproportionate lingering effects on me after I left the house. As an adult I have a reasonable diet, though, without Debbie's intervention, I tend towards off-brand, on-sale grocery purchases and canned goods. I often snack, but rarely overeat, and, at the age of 52, am only a few pounds overweight.

But that changed when Sara was born. In a reaction to how I was raised that could have been scripted by Freud – and makes me question the notion of "free will," at least in the absence of a strong dose of therapy – I responded to my mother's relationship with food by taking the opposite approach with Sara. For the first few years of her life this didn't cause problems. If she was hungry, I'd feed her, mostly high-fat content avocado. Since she was born tiny – less than five pounds – that was what the doctor had prescribed to plump her up. And until she was three or four she would eat fewer distinct items than I had fingers, limiting my ability to get into much nutrition mischief.

As she entered kindergarten Sara's sweet tooth began to grow, and my slumbering food proclivities woke up and started to run amuck. Almost every day on our walk home from school we'd stop at a corner liquor store. I'd buy Sara the junk food item of her choosing: a packet of M&Ms, Reese's Peanut Butter Cups – the four cup variety, generously gifting one to me – or, occasionally, Doritos, which she'd smash in the bag before eating, claiming that made more of them. If she had a friend with her I'd buy them similar snacks, their eyes round as they scanned the candy rack for a treat that they were probably rarely, if ever, allowed to have at home.

I say "probably" because I had no idea what Sara's friends were allowed to eat. It never crossed my mind to ask them, or call their parents to find out if it was okay for me to stuff their child with crappy food. Once, after I'd taken Sara and a couple of her pals to McDonalds, Debbie admonished me that I should have called their parents to ask their permission first.

"Why?" I asked.

"Because they might not want you to feed their kids that stuff," she answered, looking at me like I was an idiot.

"Huh," I thought to myself, immediately discounting the notion that a kid's parents should have anything to say about what they ate while they were in my charge. I was in full, oblivious, tantrum against my mother; I wasn't going to let anyone stop me from offering a child a tasty treat.

As word spread about my food exploits, I became

known among children and their parents as "the candy man," a moniker I didn't entirely dislike. Amazingly, while a mom or two would sometimes quiz me about what I'd fed her child, it was always in good humor. No one ever called me to account for why I'd allowed their son to eat an entire oversized package of Red Vines; no junk food intervention was staged.

In the meantime, Sara steadily gained weight. Debbie looked at her body as she helped her get dressed, urgently whispering to me that Sara's shape didn't look healthy. Finally, as if having an epiphany of her own, she started regularly interrogating me about what snacks I'd fed Sara that day. I tried to fend her off, arguing that chocolate was a healthy treat, and that Sara's body was doing what came naturally. Debbie persisted; her complaints morphing into my mother's voice deep within my lizard brain.

It took a few years, but slowly, as if I'd crawled out of Plato's cave, rubbing my eyes as I blinked into the light, I began to see that feeding Sara an afterschool Lunchables, hand-picked by her at 7-11 twice a week, wasn't good parenting. By the time Sara was nine, I'd mostly righted myself and more often than not acted sensibly around her food choices.

At the same time I freed myself from my childhood food bonds, Sara's interest in sweets diminished. While before she'd beg me for a sugary snack, and have a tantrum if I didn't serve it up, she increasingly respected my "no's." Soon, she stopped asking for candy entirely. She too had noticed that she'd gained unwelcome weight, and, as she progressed towards middle school, became more aware of good nutrition habits and her own body image. After reading *Chew On This: Everything*

You Don't Want to Know about Fast Food, she now refuses to go anywhere near a McDonalds.

Still, Sara sometimes asks me to stop at a convenience market to buy a Lunchables – though she's more intrigued by the food kit concept then the actual contents – or a bag of chips. But now I have no trouble refusing her request. Most of the time, at least.

Handbook Tips: Am I Fat?

▸ It has puzzled psychologists for decades: is there a correct answer to the query, "Am I fat?" If your daughter or wife pops that question, while examining themselves in the mirror, or, worse, looking you in the eye, experts say there's only one right answer: "Hell, no; you look great!" An actual honest response can only be rendered by an exact peer of the questioner – a 12-year-old girl responding to the same, for example – and only if significant trust has already been established.

▸ If you don't want your kid to drink cola with Cheetos-dusted hands, followed by a couple of Pop-Tarts for dessert, then start thinking about weaning yourself off these substances, replaced with organically-raised kale, or an array of seeds and nuts. Monkey see, monkey obsessively replicate. You can always eat the forbidden foods when you're out and about without them. Just remember not to leave any tell-tale wrappers in your car; I've been busted by Sara more than once after dining at a fast-food restaurant.

▶ Don't make food into a fetish, but do make it special. A donut with sprinkles every once in a while, or a SpongeBob-shaped popsicle; it's all good, particularly if you're celebrating something with your child. Eating is every day; junk food or sweets is a celebratory thing.

Nature

Growing up in Southern California – and later in the Bay Area – my three sisters and brother – a late-addition to my parent's brood, who was born when I was 13 years old – would ride our bikes, walk to school, or play in the dry creek beds near our house without a second thought. Many long-time Californians experienced this same childhood freedom, exploring marshes before they were turned into tract homes or industrial parks, and rolling down undeveloped hillsides. Youth was spent biking to friends' houses, investigating tadpoles in meandering creeks, searching for fossils, arrowheads, or old bottles, and playing hide-and-seek in wide open fields, sometimes with just the thick fog to hide us.

Today, children growing-up in cities do none of these things, at least not unsupervised. Much of San Francisco's open space, including the vacant lots that used to dot every neighborhood, has been paved over. Many, maybe most, parents wouldn't let their kids play alone in an urban park, or bike much farther than the nearest corner.

When we lived in the same San Francisco neighborhood as my brother and his family, Debbie and I frequently discussed how old Sara would have to be to walk by herself the 10 blocks to visit her cousin, Olivia, who is less than six months younger than her. We moved before she turned 10, but that wasn't yet old enough for us. After she turned 11 we gave Sara permission to visit Dolores Park – much of which we can see from our house – as long as she's with at least one friend. But Olivia isn't allowed to go there without adult supervision.

Relative to even a generation ago, our children's sense of freedom and familiarity with nature has been substantially diminished. Low-income children living in the state's urban areas may never see a redwood tree, or dip their toes in the Pacific Ocean. Even upper income families' interaction with nature is often limited to tightly supervised nature walks and highly scheduled camping trips. In San Francisco, at least, gone are the long days when a pair of adolescents could spend hours wandering along a quasi-urban stream, occasionally squatting down to poke a stick into a leaf, or stare at an unusual-looking beetle.

This loss coincides with a period in which urban society's relationship with nature tends to center on divisions over who gets to use what amount of scarce open space for which activities. Dog walkers – often paid professionals – herd up to a half-dozen free range canines into available patches; preservationists try to fence off tracts to be populated by native

flora and fauna only; soccer players, ultimate Frisbee gamers, roller skaters, and mountain bikers all vie for their part of what's left of paradise. Meanwhile, by and large, once children have graduated from whatever plastic playgrounds are available to them they're kept away from experiencing the urban eco-system entirely. Nature is found at the zoo, or behind glass walls at a museum.

Debbie and my attempts to help Sara develop a healthy relationship with nature mostly revolve around the ocean. Almost since she was born we've taken her tide pooling, scrambling along shoreline rocks, searching for sea creatures. At first she'd protest, and want to be carried, or balked at stepping from rock to rock unless I tightly held her hand. But now she vies to lead our expeditions, racing to be the first one to spot a star fish.

City living has always been full of trades-offs. While we can't swim in the local watering hole we do have access to superlative art, science, and natural history museums, multiple live theaters, and, though struggling, a public transportation system. San Francisco children who don't have unbridled access to nature can learn about art at multiple museums, dance at the ballet, and experience the symphony. While our kids may not have the same intimacy with nature as their country cousins, they might be better off than their suburban counterparts, who grow up in a middle ground where nature principally consists of manicured lawns, and culture is found at the mall or multiplex.

We may never again experience the childhood freedoms we had a generation ago. But we can provide our children with a sense that they live in a place that consists of more than buildings, asphalt roads, swing sets, and street trees. If we don't, we risk replicating half-millennium old attitudes towards nature, in which a walk in the woods is a scary thing to do, and quiet contemplation sitting on a boulder next to a stream is forever replaced by the restless chatter of video games and social media.

Handbook Tips: Redefining Nature

▸ Take a nature hike, in your own home. Tell your child you want to visit a jungle, but first need to prepare some supplies: a magnifying glass and flashlight. When you've gathered everything together, gesture for them to follow you…to the kitchen pantry! Using the flashlight, search out products that only contain natural ingredients, with no elements listed that you don't immediately recognize. The next frontier, if you're bold; the bathroom, where you can examine where water comes from and speculate on where it goes; if you're lucky, you'll discover a stash of mold!

▸ No matter where you live, there's vegetation right outside your door. I can see more than five shades of green from the window of my home office. Gather together your outside-the-house supplies – a hat, bag of snacks and expansive crayon set or color wheel flinched from a local paint store – and take a slow walk with your child around the block, stopping to match each plant's hue with the wheel or crayons. If you can't find the identical shade, you've discovered a new color species! Go ahead and name it.

▶ If you're ambitious, repeat the above, but bring along a camera. Snap a photograph of each plant you encounter. At home research the name of the plant, and create a map diagramming where each species is located, and some basic facts about it.

Paid Mommy

I was driving Sara home from school after several days of suffering from a bad cold, which Sara hadn't contracted.

"Gilda sure is smart," said Sara, referring to her nanny.

"What do you mean," I asked.

"I haven't gotten your cold," Sara replied, "cause of Gilda!"

One of Gilda's philosophies was that, in a time in which bottles of hand sanitizers are as common as flies once were, children should be allowed to get dirty. Dirty; not filthy. She carefully policed public toilets for Sara – wiping down the seat, and double-wrapping the paper coverings – but believed that happy interactions with out-in-the-world dirt helped build a child's immune system.

While other moms or nannies rushed to wipe their charges' hands after they'd picked up a toy left behind in a playground sandbox, Gilda would patiently wait until Sara was done playing before cleaning her up. Recent studies have proven Gilda right: researchers have concluded that the bacteria that enters the body along with dirt spur the development of a health immune system. Sara suffered through some significant illnesses during her first few years, but those were probably because of her small size and some bad parenting decisions. Since reaching school age Sara has been remarkably healthy.

Gilda was in her late-50s when my and another family hired her to take care of our two new babies. She'd emigrated from Guatemala when she was a teenager, first working as a janitor at San Francisco International Airport, before shifting to changing diapers at preschools, and finally setting up her own informal day care business. When we first met her she was recently separated from her husband after raising three children of her own.

Gilda taught Debbie and I how to be better parents, and treated Sara like she was her granddaughter. Debbie and I called her "paid mommy," though Debbie was careful never to hand Gilda money in front of Sara, wanting to preserve our daughter's sense that she was a loving adopted grandmother who cared for her when her parents were working, rather than just a hired hand.

A gentle, religious, soul, Gilda is quick with a quip. After returning with Sara from a bus ride to the park, where the pair witnessed the usual rough-around-the-edges interactions between passengers, she remarked, with a smile, "the only problem with public transportation, is the public." And when we'd thank her for nurturing our daughter, she'd joke that she took care of Sara for free; she just charged us for pushing the stroller up and down San Francisco's steep hills.

At the end of the work day – hers and ours – I'd often drive Gilda to a Bay Area Rapid Transit station, where she'd catch a train to her home in Richmond, 20 miles away and across the San Francisco Bay. She'd tell me stories about Sara, focusing on something courageous, funny, or talented my daughter had done that day.

"What do you like best about your job?" I once asked her.

"The best part is when the children are happy, that's the best part," she said. "They make me happy."

Her parting words to me or my wife were almost always the same, "Thank you for letting me love Sara. Thank you."

"No, thank you!" I'd respond. But by then she was on her way.

Handbook Tips: Extended Family
- ▸ Some parents feel guilty that they have to place their child in the care of someone else; Debbie and I saw it as an opportunity. For her first two years we took turns schlepping Sara to my mom's house most workdays, an hour and half round trip journey. Our friend, Chris – large, bald, and heavily tattooed – who commuted in that direction took one of the shifts. It was a double-blessing, allowing baby Sara to spend time with my mother and with a friend she now considers a godparent.

Walk Like a Man

My step-grandfather, Walter, taught me how to walk. Not in the sense of helping me with my first wobbly steps, but in the form of the long urban walks that have become one of my primary means of transportation and exercise. Every day Walter, usually accompanied by my grandmother, Sara – my daugher's namesake – would walk a long circuit around their San Diego neighborhood. Only a hard rain could keep them from their appointed rounds.

Walter walked for the exercise, and as a kind of scouting mission for valuable junk. To survive during the Great Depression, he'd scoured under stadium seats after games, searching for lost change, a habit he retained all his life. He returned from his walks with smatterings of objects in serviceable shape – nuts, bolts, nails, washers, bent metal, coins, books, dolls without arms and toys imprinted with tire marks – which he'd recondition, reuse, or carefully store for future use. Once, over several trips, he brought home a pile of discarded wood scraps, which he fashioned into blocks that his grandchildren played with throughout our childhoods; enough to build small forts. A few buckets of blocks continue to survive, played with by Sara and her cousins.

Sometimes, when my three sisters and I stayed with them during our twice yearly pilgrimages, one of us would tag along with Walter while Sara managed the others. He'd take me or my little sister in a stroller, our short legs unable to keep pace with his determined strides. Every few months he'd replace the worn-down, one-inch long, kidney-shaped metal protectors he hammered into his shoes' heel, with a smaller one attached under the toe. The steel bits caused a tell-tale tapping sound, which my grandfather's gait translated into a comforting metallic scuffling noise. To my young eyes the work – the shoe held tightly in a vise as Walter detached the old piece with a slender chisel, and pounded in a new strip using tiny nails – felt like a prayer. A blessing for the shoes: you take care of them, they'll take care of you.

Over the years Walter and Sara, dressed in coordinated turquoise or white sweaters or jackets, with matching hats, became minor celebrities along their route. Urban legends, in the same constellation as Bill Petter, who, attired in a red coat and big white overstuffed gloves, waved at passing cars in his Washington State neighborhood for a quarter century; or Marian and Vivian Brown, twins who strolled downtown San Francisco in identical bright snappy outfits with hats atop their meticulously coiffed hair. It was Sara who dressed them, in proud display of a late life partnership in which she was responsible for food and comfort, while Walter took care of money and shelter.

When I was a teenager my grandparents moved from San Diego to Palo Alto, to be closer to my parents. They stopped walking, and then, not so long afterwards, stopped living. Eventually, I followed in their footsteps, though I don't wear white or turquoise, and rarely don a hat. But I'm still relatively young; there's time for that.

In my early-20s my then brother-in-law, Larry, a part-time forest ranger, told me that Pivetta made the best hiking boots. I bought a pair. For the next 20 years I intermittently tramped the United States, and the world, in my Pivettas. They carried me to what was still Yugoslavia, where a worker at a hostel I was staying at told me that things weren't what they seemed. I danced with them in an underground bunker on a kibbutz near the Lebanese border, as Israeli jets screamed northward overhead, on bombing missions. I used them to climb a small mountain on a Greek Island. At the top, I found a pack of cigarettes and a lighter carefully stowed between rocks by a previous visitor. Though a social smoker at best, I lit a gifted stick, savoring it in gratitude for those who came before me.

In graduate school in Michigan, I walked through drifting snow to and from my classes, a Californian mesmerized by the frosted trees. During the 1980s, I strolled from my shared house near a heroin distribution node in Northeast Washington D.C., down 14th Street, past the hookers recovering from their night shifts in 24-hour donut shops, through Lafayette

Park, to my job at the New Executive Office Building, across from the White House. The walk was a kind of passageway, in which I'd travel through D.C.'s lingering race-based economic devastation to the NEOB's Secret Service-staffed security portal, which featured a gigantic portrait of Ronald Reagan beaming his insistent optimism down from an adjacent wall. It may have been morning in America, but my daily walk told me that, at least in some places, it was more akin to the morning after.

Walking is a humbling experience. Where my grandfather found objects, I'd find humility, entertainment, and, sometimes, wisdom. When Sara was just a week old, Debbie and I strollered her from our flat on Potrero Hill through the Mission District to Dolores Park to see the San Francisco Mime Troupe. Proud of our urban adventure, we arrived back home a few hours later to discover that Sara's new skin was alarmingly sunburned. Our wannabe hipster pride knocked aside by a reminder to pay attention.

Running for City Supervisor at the end of this century's first decade, I walked miles daily, knocking on doors answered by people with stories to tell about their neighborhoods, and their lives. A Latina mom shared her concerns that municipal budget cuts left her teenage daughter with nothing to do over the summer, subject to the urgent whispers of drugs and gangs; an African-American man told me that my decade living and working in the community made me a newcomer, insufficiently rooted to represent his community; another Black man described how he'd bought his home in the formerly predominately African-American Bayview neighborhood after, almost a half-century earlier, real estate redlining chased him away from virtually every other San Francisco neighborhood. Though I didn't win, it was the best part of my campaign: finding people's stories, sometimes twisted by time or bruised with emotion, given away freely at their stoops. And as a result of all that walking, up steep hills and back down, I lost five pounds.

Recently, after a period of professional drift, I had a dream in which I'd misplaced my shoes at a party. Hard as I looked, I couldn't find them, despite help from a friendly acquaintance.

"I guess you'll have to walk home in your socks," she said.

And, in my dream, I did. But I knew both in my dream and when I awoke, that I'd become too physically and intellectually sedentary. It was time to find my boots, strap them on, and start walking.

Handbook Tips: Walk Like a Baby

▸ On urban hikes Debbie favors a quick stride directly to our destination. I prefer a slower stroll, and, if we have time, like to choose different streets on which to amble, to see new things. Sara's post-toddler technique was even more leisurely: she'd sit on almost every stoop we came across, often giggling to herself, as if testing out the cement, tile, or marble steps to see if she wanted to take them home. Everyone has a different pace; families need to accommodate one another.

▸ As a pre-teen Sara now maps out our walks, often driven by nostalgia to visit her former elementary school or a favorite park, or as part of a restaurant outing. Debbie and I are happy to follow her path.

Next

My extended family believes that the truth should never get in the way of telling a good story. Even the most mundane activity can be hyped to fairytale levels.

Several years ago Debbie, Sara, and my then 16-year-old nephew, Elias, were at the end of a stay in Niger, West Africa, where I was working on a government reform project. Hours before we were to depart our flight was canceled; the plane had broken down in Mali. We were re-scheduled to leave the next day. The rumor that spread through my family back in the states: we'd missed our flight, and may be stuck in Niger for a week.

My family's embellishments are a way to "sell papers." It's the attention-grabbing headlines that move product, or, in my family's case, garner interest from others. There's no need to fact-check, since either the hyperbole will ultimately be deflated by the principle players, or the story will fade as the family news cycle shifts to the next headline.

News is always deeply influenced by who's telling the story. While in Niger I lent my car and driver to Debbie, Sara, and Elias. We had a mix-up in communication, and they came to pick me up at the office where I was working, while I'd already caught a ride home. When we finally met-up, Debbie, frustrated by the experience, said they'd been waiting a half-hour for me at the office. No, it'd only been 10 minutes, retorted my nephew. I asked my driver, Sidi, how long they'd waited.

"Fifteen or 20 minutes," he said.

I was tempted to believe Sidi; as a driver he was a professional waiter, accustomed to standing-by as his clients conducted their business. But then I thought about it. Perhaps in a reaction to my family's more typical hyperbole, Elias' *always* downplayed things; Debbie tended towards more expansive storytelling. Sidi's inclination – shared by many Nigeriens – was toward peaceful compromise. Splitting the difference between Elias' and Debbie's assertions, accurate or not, was in perfect keeping with his approach to storytelling.

Sometimes accuracy matters, other times it's more important to hear a good story. Early in our relationship, I'd regularly interrupt Debbie in the middle of an anecdote that involved me with a fact check – it hadn't really been that crowded, it wasn't quite that hot, we'd walked less than that – something our friend, Chris, a tall-teller of equal stature as

Debbie, couldn't abide.

"Steven! Stop interrupting!" he'd say.

"But what she's saying isn't true," I'd reply.

"Why should that matter? It's a great story!" he'd insist. "Don't get in the way of the story!"

At a dinner with Debbie's cousin, Rhonda, my wife left the table to clear the dishes after telling an expansive yarn.

"Wow, that really cost a lot of money," Rhonda said, referring to a key element in Debbie's tale.

"Well," I said, "It wasn't quite that much. With Debbie you generally have to cut things in half."

Rhonda squinted at me, and reflected. "That sounds about right," she nodded.

As we stumble through life we ultimately discover where to go when we need accurate information, and with whom to talk when we want engaging infotainment. I'll never know exactly how long my family waited for me in Niger, but I got their messages: Debbie wanted better communication, Elias wanted to demonstrate his loyalty and patience, and Sidi wanted peace. Sometimes facts are important, but more often than not it's the meaning of things that really matters.

Ever since Sara could hold two objects in her hands she's been play acting stories. When she was two she'd take a rubber band and a crumpled piece of paper and animate them, giving them voices, and taking them on invented adventures. She loved being read to, and quickly became a television addict,

preferring shows that had strong plot lines and reoccurring characters, though, in her opinion, almost any TV was better than none. At the precipice of becoming a teenager, she still plays with her stuffed and plastic animals, creating small worlds that she directs.

When she was small, at bedtime, after I'd read a handful of picture books to her, she'd ask me to tell her a made-up a story. At first I'd come up with the characters and narrative; for at least a year the "Poopy Family," starred in a series of escapades involving being flushed down the toilet to strange lands, where they'd struggle to get home. As she got older she'd insist on identifying the characters for each night's story. Simba and Nala were frequent requests after we saw *The Lion King*.

When Sara was seven, we shifted to taking turns telling a bedtime story, in a game we called, "Next." The rules were simple. Sara identified the story's characters – three dogs, for example, or a brother and a sister – as well as their names. At first these were long and complicated – "Nesrahmeannockerbocker," or the like – but shifted to "Bob" or "Joanne" after it became clear that neither one us could remember three syllable names for more than a minute. Then she'd set the basic scene; brothers Ralph and Matt, bears, were walking to school, when they encountered Lisa, a dog, who they didn't like. I'd take it from there, starting the story off with a minute or two of narrative, after which I'd say, "next" – preferably in a nasally growl – and she'd take over. We'd bat the story between us for a dozen rounds, and then wrap things up for the evening.

Sometimes Debbie would join us, though she readily admitted that she wasn't good at the game, quickly forgetting the basic plot, or even simple character names. Occasionally she'd fall asleep in the middle of a story.

Sara and I would often allow an especially intriguing storyline to unfold over several days, or even a week or two, before we'd end things. Or, if we got sick of a set of characters, or bored with how things were going, we'd finish abruptly in ways that, if not fully satisfying, were at least done. A favorite *coup de grace* to a story going in the wrong direction, or not going at all, was one of us saying "The…Next," with the other responding "End…"

The evolution of Sara's and my storytelling practices isn't so different from how life actually unfolds. After babies are born they're introduced to various characters – mom, dad, grandma, grandpa, relatives and friends – who interact in different settings mostly chosen by the parents. At first the baby watches as the story unfolds in front of them – is told to them – their part limited to triggering activities around their basic needs: feeding, diaper-changing, comforting, though they quickly understand that they have the power to make things happen by simply smiling, or burping. Their physical demands mark their first attempts to muscle into the larger narrative, which, for their parents and everyone around them, has been going on well before they arrived, though baby doesn't know that, and, in any event, would be slow to admit to it.

The tables are already turning on my family's storytelling practices. At age eleven Sara is increasingly telling me her own stories, sometimes trying to mask them as something she actually experienced, or a true tale she heard from a friend.

Occasionally, I'll be the one calling out the characters for her to enliven, though I try to nudge her towards nonfiction, by naming her friends or teachers. I'm more interested in what really happens in her life than make believe.

I know that as she reaches her teenage years and into adulthood she'll ultimately be the one identifying the characters in her story, and triggering the plot lines. Still, I hope we continue to play next, real and fictional, for years to come. Though I know my role will diminish, I'm eager to at least maintain guest star status.

Handbook Tips: Telling Tales

- As a baby grows into a toddler, and then a preschooler, she'll start to have her own adventures, and introduce new plotlines and characters into the stories she tells: her teachers, the friends she makes and their parents. These new personalities may even become the dominate characters in a family's evolving narrative.

- Sometimes, the purportedly non-fiction stories kids tell about their day aren't true at all. In kindergarten Sara's friend Joe would convey an outrageous schoolyard incident so confidently that his parents would call us to ask if it'd actually happened. Most of the time it didn't. As she got older Sara's true accounts also increasingly morphed into complex tall tales. When called on it she'd readily admit the fiction. Perhaps she'll grow up to be a politician.

▸ Regardless of the veracity, storytelling keeps lines of communication, as well as creativity, open. It's a good habit to develop.

Who's Your Daddy?

Sara wants me to be a different type of dad. Not entirely; she fiercely loves me. But, almost since she could string seven words together into a sentence, she's lobbied me to watch more sports, be more athletic, and have more friends.

She sets up her conversations about the topic like a jail house lawyer, first establishing the facts, and then going in for the kill.

"Dad, do you like sports?" Sara asked.

"Sure," I responded.

"Then why don't you watch them more on TV?" she parried.

Or,

"Dad,"

"Yes?"

"You know Sophia's dad?" referring to her friend's

father, who, always seems to have just finished, or is about to begin, a triathlon, except without the sweat.

"Yep,"

"How come you can't be more sporty, like him?

It's true that I don't watch sports much, and my attendance at professional or college games is driven by invitations from friends, or, in the case of baseball, the couple of times Sara's school choir sang the national anthem at AT&T Park. But whenever I take her to a baseball game she quickly grows restless, and, after she's had her fill of ballpark concessions, spends most of her time at the giant slide.

While I'm no triathlete, I often bicycle up and down San Francisco's hills, use a rowing machine I recently purchased, and am a regular at my neighborhood Pilates studio. Still, none of this fulfills my daughter's vision of what a fully-functioning father should look like, which apparently best manifests as a muscular, spandex-clad jock who spends equal amounts of time on the playing fields as he does watching them on television, most likely with a bowl of Doritos within reaching distance, which he shares generously with his daughter.

Recently, I stopped to chat with one of the dads at Sara's school after I'd picked her up. We said our goodbyes, and got into the car.

"Dad, how come you don't like any of the dads at school?"

"What do you mean, I do like other dads."

"But you're not friends with any of them. You never go out with them."

"Sure I do," I responded, and named several dads with whom I'd had dinner, though mostly as part of couple's outings.

I could count maybe four school dads, if I was being generous, who I might call and ask out for a beer or the like. The truth is, like many 50-something men, while I have a few good friends, I'd cultivated the majority of them over a lifetime. Many of them live in different states, thousands of miles away. But I rarely see even my close buddies who live a few blocks from my house, and almost never speak to them on the phone. I don't have an easy explanation for this behavior, though I know it's not unusual among my peers.

Sara seemed surprised, and at least temporarily satisfied, with my answer. But I wasn't. While being sportier wasn't high on my daddy-to-do list, deepening my relationships with my friends, and making a few new ones, was prominent on my being a better man list. Sara's questioning prompted me to work on that. Lately, I've been inviting my pals, new and old, to sporting and other events. I haven't told Sara that, though. She'd only use it against me.

Magic Flutes

Until we were in our mid-teens, and lost interest, every summer my three sisters and I would visit my grandma, Sara, my daughter's namesake, and step-grandfather, Walter, in San Diego. The city had exactly the right attractions for us: sunny weather, the zoo, beaches, well-tended parks.

Walter didn't talk much, but had a sturdy, comforting presence. He spoke with his hands, which were always fixing things with calm competence. Though difficult with other adults, to her grandchildren Sara was magical. She'd have us crowd around a Jell-O mold just before taking off the large, scalloped, donut-shaped tin. At her prompting we'd all shout "Abracadabra!" She'd lift the mold, leaving behind a fruit-laden ring of Jell-O, the perfection of which she'd quickly credit to how well we'd said the essential incantation.

"Without your magic it wouldn't come out right," she'd

smile.

Sara and Walter's house was at the bottom of a small hill, the view from which, as we drove down it in Walter's Lincoln, was sufficiently spectacular for one of us to utter on an early visit, "Oh, grandpa, what a view!" Sara would repeat that phrase every time we drove down that hill, encouraging us to do the same, in a kind of joyful prayer.

Their backyard – a carefully tended desert garden crisscrossed with agate-strewn paths – looked out over an undeveloped, brush-filled canyon. As we grew into adolescence this mini-gorge became increasingly intriguing. We'd peer over the backyard's edge, searching the crevices for lizards, snakes, and rodents.

Sara, however, thought that the canyon served as a hideout for bandits and miscreants. "Promise me you won't go down there," Sara admonished us. "It's not safe."

So, of course, on one summer visit, we did. We told Sara that we were going outside to play, walked around the block, and straight down into the canyon. It held narrow dirt pathways winding through clumps of sagebrush, with smatterings of trash, crumbling rock and the occasional scurrying lizard. We loved it, and planned to return soon.

The next morning, Sara told us she had something for us. "Flutes!" she said, passing a wooden toy flute to each of us. "Just only play them outside."

Out we went, tooting our flutes, up the street, around the block, and down into the canyon. We marched, single-filed, through the windy dirt paths, releasing random fluty notes to float into the clouds. Soon enough, we heard a voice above us.

"I can hear you down there!" called Sara, from her backyard, "I told you not to go in the canyon!"

Sheepishly we marched back home, clutching our lifeless instruments in our hands. We never went to the canyon again. But we did get to keep the flutes.

Handbook Tips: Maintaining the Magic

▸ One of the best things about childhood is believing in magic – Santa Claus, the Tooth Fairy, unseen forest creatures – and one of the worst things about adulthood is the loss of those beliefs. Although you can only maintain the fiction of made-up creatures so long, magic of a different kind can be fostered. Noticing a set of drifting clouds or whispering winds can be enchanting, as can the retelling of dreams in which impossible things can happen.

▸ Our children enter into a world of magical technology – smartphones, television, air travel – that's made real many of our centuries-old fanciful stories, of flying carpets, long-distant telepathy, and three-dimensional imagery. Magic is all around us.

Parental Sins

"Hey Daddy, can I have a play date?" Sara asked me, as I picked her up from a summer camp for nine-year-olds held at an elementary school.

"With who?" I asked. She pointed to a brown hair girl wearing a blue skirt, who was sitting on the steps leading into the facility.

"Uh, sure," I said, as we walked over to the girl. "What's your name?" I asked her.

"Chloe," she smiled back.

"Who's picking you up?"

"My dad," she said, "But sometimes he's late."

"Okay, we'll wait with you," I said.

As we waited, the two girls whispered to each other, sitting close. I looked at my cellphone. It was 10 minutes past pick-up time. A few kids were playing tag in front of the school while their parents chatted. Most of the day campers had already left. I looked at Chloe. She didn't seem upset that her father hadn't yet appeared. As I played with my phone, a disheveled looking man, wearing a frayed corduroy sport coat and khaki pants that needed a wash, hurried towards us. For a moment I thought he was homeless, and was going to ask me for some spare change.

"Hey Chloe," the man said.

"Hi, Dad!" Chloe got up and gave her father a hug.

"Hello," I said, "I'm Steven. Our daughters seem to have taken a shine to one another."

"Hey, I'm Steve," Steve grinned back at me. "Good name you have there."

We nodded at each other idiotically, in the way fathers sometimes do when they're temporarily forced together by their daughters.

"So, these two want to have a play date," I said. "Should we exchange numbers so we can arrange that sometime?"

"You can take her right now," said Steve. "What do you say, Chloe?"

"Yes!" shouted Chloe. She and Sara started jumping up and down, squealing and holding hands.

"Okay, I guess that's alright. We live in Potrero Hill; right on the corner at Vermont and 18th streets."

"Yeah, Yeah, I know where that is. There's a dry cleaner on the corner, right?"

"Yep," I said. "We're across the street from it. Maybe you can pick her up around 5?"

"Sounds good," said Steve. "Here, Chloe, take my

phone." He handed her his cell phone. "Call me at home if you need anything." He hugged his daughter, and started to walk away.

"Don't you want my number?" I called after him.

"No need. Chloe has my cell!" he said, and strode away.

Sara and Chloe had a great time, playing with Sara's toys, and sharing secrets. When Debbie came home from work just before 5 o'clock, I introduced her to Chloe.

"Is she staying for dinner?" Debbie asked me

"No. Her dad is picking her up any time now."

5 o'clock turned to 5:15, and then 5:30.

"Why don't you call him?" Debbie asked.

"He didn't give me his number," I said.

"He didn't give you his number? That's weird. Do you know this guy?"

"I met him for the first time today," I said. "He gave Chloe his cell phone; she can call her home number."

Chloe called home. No one answered. At 5:45 Debbie decided to feed the girls macaroni and cheese. They'd just finished, at around 6:30, when the doorbell rang. I opened the door, and in burst Steve with a chubby woman with frizzy hair.

"Hi," said the woman loudly, "I'm Chloe's mother, Ellen." Ellen marched into the house. "Wow, nice place." She strode past the living room, kitchen and dining room, and sat down on the family room sofa. Steve followed, sat next to her, and put his arm around her shoulder. They asked us where Sara went to school, and told us where Chloe attended.

Not knowing what else to do, I sat down in the chair

next to the couple. Debbie remained standing. Both of us were irritated. We didn't know these people, who seemed oblivious that they'd come to pick-up their daughter an hour and a half after I'd ask Steve to do so, and couldn't be reached in the meantime. Plus, Steve had an odd air to him, and Ellen was aggressive, pointedly probing how Sara got into her school and asking how much we paid in rent. We wanted them to leave. More than 20 minutes passed before they finally did.

"We'll need to have Sara over for a play date," Steve said, as I walked him to the door.

"Yeah, sure," I mumbled.

"I don't want Sara to be friends with that girl," Debbie said. Chloe and Sara had had another great day together at camp, and Sara wanted us to arrange a play date at Chloe's house. "I don't like her parents."

"You can't let children suffer for the sins of their parents," I replied. It was an adage I often employed when Debbie balked at arranging play dates with a child whose parents were unpleasant. And I believed it. I'd known enough kids growing up that didn't have lunch money, or whose clothes weren't washed, to understand the challenges children face if their parents are socially awkward, neglectful or absent. My own mom and dad tended towards social isolation when I was growing up, which had sometimes embarrassed me, and made it difficult to maintain friendships.

"Okay, you call them then. I'm not getting involved."

Chloe had given me her home number after camp that day. I dialed it. Ellen answered. She said Sara would be welcome to come over after camp the next day. She gave me their address, which was near the camp. Ellen readily agreed to my offer to pick-up Chloe and Sara and bring them to her house.

The next day after camp I walked the girls up the stairs to Chloe's second floor flat and rang the doorbell. There was no response. The girls sat on the steps. I rang again, and then again. A few more minutes passed, when Steve finally opened the door.

"Hey," he said. "I was taking a nap. Come on in."

We walked into a narrow hallway that was choked with guitars, some in cases, most not.

"Come on!" Chloe shouted to Sara, and tugged her down the hall.

"You like guitars," I said to Steve's back, as he walked towards what turned out to be the kitchen.

"I sell them," he said. "That's how I make a living. You want a drink?"

"No thanks," I said. "I gotta get back to work. I'll come get her around 5 o'clock." I walked past the kitchen to a small room behind it, crowded with household items, where Sara and Chloe were playing on the floor.

"See you later, Pumpkin," I knelt down and hugged Sara.

"Bye, Dad," Sara said, without looking up.

At 5, I was back at Chloe's house, ringing the doorbell. No one answered. I walked back down the stairs, to a wooden fence that shielded the side yard, and peered over, thinking they might be in the back somewhere. I saw a patch of dried grass, lined by concrete, a deflated red rubber ball in one corner, but no girls. I walked back up the steps, rang the bell, and turned towards the street. I saw Steve striding my way, clutching a small bag.

"Hey," he said.

"Where are the girls?" I asked.

"Inside. I had to run an errand. I told them not to answer the door while I was out."

I stared at him, and said nothing. He didn't seem to notice, or care. After he opened the door, I called out to Sara. She emerged from the back of the house.

"Bye, Chloe," she shouted over her shoulder, as she strolled down the hall towards me.

"How was the play date?" I asked her, after we'd put our seat belts on, and pulled away from the curb.

"It was fun," she said.

"How long was Steve gone?"

"I dunno. Maybe an hour."

I grimaced at her in the rear-view mirror, but she was looking out the window at a dog being walked by its owner. At home I told Debbie about Steve's absence.

"We don't let Sara stay home alone at our house. Why should we allow it with those people, who we don't even like?" she asked, crossly. "She's never going over there again," she insisted.

"Don't punish the child…" I started to say, without much conviction.

"Don't give me that. We need to make sure Sara is safe. She and Chloe are only nine years old; they shouldn't be left alone. They can have play dates at our house, but only if you arrange it," Debbie said firmly, adding, perhaps unnecessarily, "I'm not talking to those people."

"Okay," I said. Both of us knew that it was unlikely I'd make any play date arrangements. Debbie was Sara's social scheduler, a role I played only reluctantly. Still, I believed in my adage, and wanted Sara and Chloe to have a chance to be friends, if that's what they wanted, regardless of what we thought about her parents.

That summer I arranged two more play dates with Chloe. When I called, Ellen would offer to have the girls at her house, but quickly agreed when I countered that it'd be easy for me to pick-up Chloe and bring her to our house, and then drop her back off at theirs. But my interactions with Steve, who never seemed to leave the house, unless his daughter was home, didn't get any easier. During the few moments when I'd hand off Chloe he'd complain about the high cost of living in San Francisco, squinting at me like it was my fault, and ramble in ways that I couldn't follow. I started to dread our conversations.

Camp ended, and so did summer. Sara and Chloe no longer saw each other every day. Though Sara still liked her new friend, she stopped talking about her. A few weeks into the school year Ellen left me a voicemail, asking if Chloe could have a play date with Sara. I never returned it. I still feel bad about that.

Handbook Tips: Frenemies

▶ Once you've crossed into parenthood, chances are you'll leave behind many of those fun friends you made at college, work, and through social activities. If marriage didn't already separate you from your favorite running partner or gal pal, your kid almost certainly will. They just won't be all that interested in your stories about explosive diapers or soccer tournaments, and you'll be too tired to keep up with them at your previous haunts. After your kid starts preschool, she'll starting choosing who you'll hang out with. Your old friends will be replaced by the parents of your kid's friends. Like 'em or not, you'll be seeing lots of them; at school, sporting events, and play dates. Try to be nice.

▶ You'll need to learn the complicated taxonomy of today's school yard friendships. There'll be a changing roster of BFFs, friends, acquaintances, well-wishers, frenemies, and enemies, along with email, text, and virtual game buddies – who may never materialize as physical companions of your child – classmates who can be called for homework assignments, and those pesky kids who send out threatening chain emails that'll give your kid nightmares.

Dating Rules

"Um Dad..?" Sara, said.

She was sitting in the backseat of the car, as we drove home from elementary school. During the 20 minutes a day we spend in my Mini Cooper, hurling down the 280 freeway, she's especially loquacious, like a friendly stranger after their third drink at a neighborhood bar.

"Yeah, Pumpkin?"

"Oh, nothing."

"What is it?" I asked, eyeing her through the rear-view mirror.

"I really should talk to mommy about this," she paused. "There's this boy at school who I kind of have a crush on…"

"Uh, huh," I said, "Everybody gets crushes, sometimes."

"No, but, what should I do?" she blurted, exasperated. "I knew I should just talk to mom about it."

Yes, I thought, you should. "Tell me what the problem is," I said.

"Well, how do I tell him I like him? I mean, *like* like him."

"You could invite him over for a play date." Wrong thing to say, my brain shouted. I hurried on. "Or maybe next time we have tickets to something fun, like a concert, or movie, you could ask him if he wants to come along."

I could see Sara eyeing me, like I was an idiot. Which of course on this topic, I am.

"The problem is that three other girls also like him. And Lara said she has dibs."

"Dibs?" I asked, "You can't put dibs on a boy. The boy gets to decide who he wants to be friends with."

"No, no, she got dibs. She said it first," she countered, sounding like a lawyer familiar with schoolyard ordinances.

"Hmm," I replied. I searched for something to say. I came up empty. For a few moments the car was quiet but for the swooshing sounds of high-speed travel in the background.

Sara broke the silence. "I don't think I'm ready yet," she said. "I'll just wait until fifth grade."

"Sounds good," I said, battling my desire to pump my fist and shout, "Yes!" "You'll know when you're ready. There's no hurry."

The next day after school, we were walking to the Mini.

"It's going well with my crush. We're talking with each other," she said, in a voice that suggested this was the beginning and the end of the conversation.

"That's good," I said. I got into the car and buckled

my seat belt. We pulled out of the parking lot, and picked up speed. Sara gazed out the window.

"Can we go to Jackson Park? I want to play on the monkey bars."

I smiled, relieved that Sara still had one foot firmly in a childhood where boys weren't yet an all-consuming distraction.

"Sure," I said, as we slowed for a traffic light. I'll take you wherever you want to go."

Handbook Tips: Dating

- When talking to your child about their budding "relationships," it's best to approach them as if they were an untamed animal. Don't raise the subject yourself, but rather subtly encourage it by asking more broadly about "their day," with such soft probes as "make any new friends?" Don't look them in the eyes when they're chatting about it, and don't express any overt enthusiasm about the topic. Stay cool, like you're trying to catch a glimpse of skittish unicorn in an imaginary forest. Feel grateful if you see something from the corner of your eyes.

- Crushes come, and crushes go. Don't spend too much energy trying to remember who your kid "like likes" today; tomorrow it'll be someone else.

- You, dad, are the central reference point for your daughter's future relationship with men. Don't blow it.

Eeyore

When I was four years old my mother gave me a handmade stuffed Eeyore for Hanukkah. He was gray, with two mismatched button eyes, and a red-stitched smile. I'm not sure why mom chose that Winnie the Pooh character for me; one of my sisters got Kanga, from the same series. Eeyore is a pessimistic, though compassionate, creature. He's a bit of a downer, the great-grandfather, perhaps, of SpongeBob SquarePants' Squidward Quincy Tentacles.

Eeyore often loses his detachable tail. In one story Owl finds the appendage and uses it as a door bell pull. Winnie the Pooh retrieves it, and Christopher Robin pins the tail back on Eeyore, in a riff on the once popular birthday party game.

I was delighted with the gift, which became one of my most prized possessions, not least because it was a handcrafted expression of love from my otherwise mostly remote mother.

I kept Eeyore throughout my childhood. He followed me to college and into adulthood. When I was single he'd live on my bed, though I won't admit to actually cuddling him. Otherwise, he'd lean against a shelf somewhere. Through many moves across the United States, multiple girlfriends, marriage, and Sara's birth, Eeyore stayed with me, a steadily fading and flattening but recognizable talisman from my childhood.

A few years ago, Debbie, Sara, and I moved to a new home in San Francisco. After the boxes were unpacked, and everything put away, something was missing. Eeyore. I looked everywhere for him, even returning to our old house and searching the backyard. He couldn't be found.

His loss bruised my heart. I quietly mourned him like an old friend had died. Sara, who'd played with Eeyore occasionally, picked up on my pain, and, in the ensuing years, periodically encouraged me not to give up hope, to keep up the search; Eeyore would be found. But I knew he was gone.

When Sara was 10 she visited Debbie's mom in Palm Desert, with plans to go to Disneyland. She asked me for some pocket money to buy presents, including for me and Debbie.

"What should I buy you?" Sara asked.

"I dunno. Maybe one of those little viewfinder things, that you can look through and see scenes of Disneyland." I said.

Her grimace amply communicated that she thought that was a lame gift idea. "I know what I'm going to get," Sara said, switching to a secret smile. "You'll see."

A few days later, back in San Francisco, Sara told me

to sit on the sofa and close my eyes, a gift-giving practice our family replicated from my childhood. She placed something soft and furry in my hands. I opened my eyes. It was a small, stuffed Eeyore, with a detachable tail.

"Do you like him?" Sara asked.

I looked down at the stuffy, willing myself not to cry.

"I sure do!" I said, giving her a hug. "He's perfect!"

Sara insisted that Eeyore sleep with me that night, though she also made it clear that she'd be playing with him on occasion. I was happy to share him.

In Winnie the Pooh, Eeyore's frequently misplaced tail would be found and reattached by one of his friends, making him whole. Sara did something similar for me. When I lost Eeyore, the pain I felt wasn't for the object, but for something I'd experienced long ago: a childhood moment in which I'd deeply felt my mother's love, the expression of which I couldn't often find. Sara recreated that experience for me. In a move I found both cosmically funny and deeply touching, she pinned the tail back on this old donkey.

Handbook Tips: Missing Something that No Longer Exists
- One of the more magical elements of raising a child is that you continually fall in love with a being that changes fundamentally every few years. Sure, you might see glimpses of that mischievous toddler in your emerging adolescent, but who they are – capacity to understand things, knowledge, sense of humor – is

ever-evolving. It's easy to miss that sweet-smelling baby that you held in your arms, while at the same time hugging your pre-teen daughter after a winning soccer game. It's a delicious, confusing, amazing experience.

▸ While your kid is changing, so are you, and not just your body. Nurture the positive, shed the negative.

It's a Cruel World

"It's a cruel world," my mom used to say, whenever I complained about being bored or lonely. Her tone was usually distracted, or tired, as if the world's cruelty was so well accepted that even a five year old should know all about it. In retrospect, a part of me hopes she was being ironic, or even campy, though that's improbable. My mom rarely uses irony and is never purposely campy. More likely she was repeating something she'd heard, perhaps from her mother, one of those pat parent phrases, like, "I'll pull this car over right now if you don't stop arguing," or "because I said so."

The real meaning of my mom's "it's a cruel world" mantra was that whatever usually unspecified action I wanted her to take to cure what ailed me wasn't going to happen. She wasn't going wiggle her nose like Samantha from the 1960s situation comedy *Bewitched* – or wave her wand like Harry

Potter – and create a posse of playmates for me, or even get down on her knees and play a few rounds of Sorry. The world wasn't so much cruel, as indifferent.

Given the times in which my mother grew-up – and the fact that she was struggling to raise five children on one parent's salary, compared to my one child to two working parent ratio – I can forgive her for labeling the world cruel. Two world wars, the Holocaust, flu and polio pandemics plagued her and the generation that raised her. Growing up, my mom was often left alone while her mother, Sara, accompanied her younger brother Joel on his frequent radio appearances and celebrity tours.

Joel, whose IQ clocked in at more than 200, was on the mega-popular "Quiz Kid" radio show, the "American Idol" of its time, except bigger. He talked when he was 18 months old, added and subtracted at age three, and when he was four could total the family's grocery bill faster than an adding machine. When he was seven he appeared in Hollywood movies. Any attempt my mother made to garner attention in the face of the Joel juggernaut was futile.

Worse yet, when my mother was in the hospital having my older sister, Marissa, her beloved father, Saul, collapsed shortly after he arrived to visit her. He was diagnosed with cancer, checked into that same hospital, and never left, dying days later. From my mother's perspective preparing for the worst to happen – and steeling oneself to the point of indifference – wasn't so much pessimistic as realistic.

Ten-year-old Sara is more interested in equity than

cruelty. "It's no fair!" is her common refrain, which she applies to pretty much anything she doesn't want to do, followed by "you're mean!" if she doesn't get her way.

I prefer Sara's underlying philosophy to my mother's. Though cruelty exists, I haven't experienced the world as systematically cruel, and certainly don't want to define it in that way. While Sara's view of fairness is egocentric, her insistence on it suggests that equity is an essential value, one that needs to be a critical element of any decision. And her deployment of meanness as an epithet implies that being nice is the correct norm, while being nasty is even worse than being a doofus, jerk, or stupid, her less frequently used labels for actions she doesn't like.

My mom's world, lived mostly in the last century, was often cruel on a global scale. While there have been notable exceptions, Sara's, unfolding in this one, has so far been fairer and nicer. I hope it stays that way, and she remains dedicated to equity as a core value. A just and kind planet is exactly the place I want my daughter to grow-up in, and, if necessary, to fight for.

Handbook Tips: Half Full
- ▸ Debbie's attitude is the opposite of my mother's; I call her "optimistic in the face of reality." She believes in the power of positive thinking, and goes to bed at night visualizing the broad outcomes she wants – a raise; the purchase of a new home – and usually wakes up in the morning with a smile on her face. Not all of her dreams

come true, but her persistence optimism is shared by Sara, who we call "the bounce back kid." No matter what the challenge, she gravitates towards happiness. I don't know if it's nature, or nurture, but, irritating as he can be, I'd rather my daughter emulate SpongeBob than Squidward.

▸ I first learned of the phenomenon when I took my nephews, six-year-old Elias and eight-year-old Simon, to the Marin County fair. As I watched them scream with joy as they rode *faux* planes that spun in circles and dipped up and down, I thought to my early 30-something self, "This is pretty tedious. But at least they're having fun." There must be a German word for it, like *schadenfreude;* taking pleasure in kids you love having a great time while you're stuck holding their coats, standing in 90 degree heat in a crowded amusement park, without a beer in your hand. Or worse. It's a weird sensation, feeling deeply satisfied and completely irritated simultaneously. Moms seem to get great enjoyment from this particular emotion; dad's not so much, but in today's post-modern world, you'd better get used to it.

Punch Burka Black

"Punch buggy red," Sara gleefully exclaimed from the back seat, as she hit me on the shoulder while I drove the Mini Cooper, a bit harder than I'd have liked.

"Ugh," I wheezed, in half-mock exasperation, "I need to pay more attention!"

"Punch Buggy" – which some of her friends call "Slug Bug" – is Sara's favorite car game, at least when we're driving in San Francisco. Taught to her by her cousin, Elias, who'd inherited a 1968 Volkswagen Beetle from his father, the pastime's rules are simple. When you see a Volkswagen Beetle, of any age, you shout-out "punch buggy," followed by the car's color, which allows the person to hit one of the other players, hopefully not too hard. Score can be kept, or not. Sara often adds "no punch backs!" which apparently can be countered by "Peter Pan says I can," which triggers another chant that I never remember in a game Sara almost always wins.

Several years after Sara started playing Punch Buggy, we went on a family trip to Morocco, where Debbie's mom was born. In Marrakesh, Debbie enrolled in a day-long cooking course, leaving Sara and me on our own. After hanging out at our *riad* for a while, we decided to get lunch. We made our way to *Jamaa el Fna*, the old city's main square, and found a second floor pizza restaurant with a commanding view of the plaza.

Eating our pizza, we gazed at the square, which was full of sidewalk restaurants and hawkers selling nuts and seeds, cheap toys, vegetables, clothing made in China, and henna tattoos. European and Arab tourists mixed with locals, many of whom were wearing head scarfs, with a few in full-on burkas that covered their entire body except their hands, which often had gloves on. Sometimes the burka-wearers even concealed their eyes behind dark glasses.

"Why do they do that?" asked Sara, as she munched on a pizza slice.

"What?"

"Wear those tent things?"

"They're called burkas," I said, "They're for modesty." I thought for a moment, trying to come up with an explanation that would suit a 10 year old. "Their religion tells them to cover up when they're outside their home. It makes them feel more comfortable."

We continued to eat our pizza, both of us taking in the colorful swirl of activity in the square. Abruptly, Sara reached across the table and punched my bicep.

"Punch burka red," she announced gleefully, "no punch backs."

"Huh?" I said, as Sara giggled. "Oh." I scanned the square. "Punch burka black!" I shouted, and gave Sara a tap on the shoulder.

"Where?" she asked. I pointed towards a woman covered in black, who was walking across the plaza holding hands with a small girl dressed in shorts and a t-shirt.

The game was on. We started spotting burka-clad women throughout the square, hidden in plain sight, like Where's Waldo, buying nuts, talking in small groups, selling vegetables, seemingly sunning themselves while sitting on the pavement, if that's possible while being comprehensively clothed. Sara and I traded soft hits, declaring, "Punch burka white…blue…purple…"

"There sure are a lot of burka colors," I said.

"Yeah," Sara responded.

It crossed my mind that the game might not be entirely appropriate. If a burka was a spiritual garb, was our game sacra-religious? If we were sitting in Jerusalem, overlooking the *Kotel* – Western Wall – would it be respectful to play Punch *Yarmulka*? Would *Adonai*, or *Allah*, strike us down for our transgressions?

My musings were cut short by the overwhelming number of burkas that seemed to be flooding the plaza. Now that we were looking for them, they were everywhere, in thick knots, colors both dark and vibrant, too many to count. Plus, we'd finished lunch. I signaled to the waiter, and paid the check.

We left the restaurant and were walking across the

square in the direction of our hotel when a middle-aged Moroccan woman in a head scarf grabbed Sara's hand and squirted some ink on it.

"Henna tattoo! I give the girl a beautiful henna tattoo!" she declared, as she hustled us towards a stool she'd set up nearby, while continuing to grasp Sara's hand in hers and squirting greenish looking ink on it.

Sara looked at me with pleading eyes, mouthing, "Daddy…" and drawing a finger across her throat. I followed as the woman sat Sara down and continued her work. Sara stared at me intently, grimacing. She wouldn't look at the woman. My head still stuffed with burkas, I didn't know if I should stop the woman in mid tattoo-making, or let her finish it. She sprinkled sparkly dust on the crude image she'd drawn on Sara. Before I said anything, she was done.

"Beautiful!" she said, holding up Sara's hand for me to admire. The tattoo spread up to Sara's wrist, large and ugly. "$20!"

I snapped out of my stupor. "What? $20? We didn't even want this," I protested, as Sara scuttled to my side and grabbed my arm, her mouth tightened in a frown.

"$20, that's the price," the woman insisted. After a brief argument I handed her a $5 bill. Sara and I strode quickly away, the woman loudly complaining behind us.

"Dad, why didn't you stop her," Sara angrily cried.

"I dunno," I said. "I thought maybe once she started it was better to get it done, rather than having half a tattoo."

"I hate it!" Sara declared, "shaking her arm at me. "Don't ever do that again."

"But why didn't you say something?" I lamely replied.

"I signaled you with my eyes," Sara seethed, biting off each word. "It's your job to take care of me. I can't believe you didn't stop her."

She was sullenly silent the rest of the way to the hotel.

"Punch burka yellow," I tried, weakly, as we passed a woman attired in that outfit. Sara ignored me. Perhaps we'd been caught up in some type of Karmic revenge for disrespecting the religious clothes around us. Or maybe I just didn't do my daddy duties. Either way, it took Sara several days to forgive me. Still, once we reconnected with Debbie, she quickly and gleefully taught her mom our new game. I didn't stop that, either.

Handbook Tips: Respect

▸ It's a dad's job to protect his kids from all kinds of things: unsafe traffic, poisonous plants, icky bugs. I semi-redeemed myself with Sara when, during a trip to Rwanda, I fought off a swarm of flying worms who, attracted by the light, insisted on crawling into our hotel room with a vengeance reminiscent of a horror movie. When you get a chance to be a hero to your family, seize it.

▸ Like most of us, Sara is fascinating by difference, and, as with most kids, doesn't try to hide it. She'll crane her neck to peer at especially short or large people and those in wheelchairs, and likes to stroke African-Americans' hair. I discourage staring, but, if the context seems right, encourage her to ask frank, but polite, questions to the person she's curious about. So far, everyone she's asked has been friendly, and I learn as much from the responses as she does.

Chewing Gum in the Bathtub

"No, you can't chew gum in the bathtub!" Debbie, insisted to 10-year-old Sara, who, during her weekly hour-long soak in the tub, had just made that request.

"Why?" Sara fought back.

"Um, because!" Debbie responded, which, after a pause, she amended to, "I don't know why; it's just doesn't seem right."

While perhaps less strait-jacketed than the generation before, those of us who grew up in the 1960s and '70s faced a spanking machine's worth of parental restrictions, which we've largely passed onto our children unedited. Many of these rules make a lot of sense: don't put plastic bags over your head; no playing inside empty refrigerators or freezers; and the classic, no running with scissors! Some of these instructions seem so obvious that the need to say them out loud suggests that we're raising a nation of near-idiots, who don't know better than to be jabbing a sharpened pencil into their mouths as they climb a narrow stair case. But, then again, when she was four-years-old Sara did just that, knocking out a tooth when she stumbled as she scrambled up the stairs while chewing on a sharpened pencil, point side in.

Other rules are less compelling. At a karate class Sara took when she was six, the instructor told his young students to yell "stranger danger, stranger danger!" and run away fast if someone they didn't know tried to talk to them. While I never saw that strategy in action, it seems ill-advised, both practically and philosophically. Run to where, exactly; into a crowd of other strangers? And, is a sudden flight impulse when encountering a new person the right thing to instill in our children? It's easy to imagine how that might not work out so well when they go to college parties.

And then there's the "no throwing a ball in the house" rule, which Debbie subscribes to, but I don't. It makes sense that you shouldn't throw a ball in a room full of china, but what if the room is empty, and there's nothing to break? Should inside ball throwing always be forbidden?

There are a host of parental food-related restrictions, including the rock band Pink Floyd's, "How can you have any pudding if you don't eat yer meat!?" Some of these make sense, like no snacking right before dinner, or putting limits on how much soda a kid should drink. Others are more mysterious. Why can't you have pizza or spaghetti for breakfast?

We still don't let Sara chew gum in the bathtub, though neither Debbie nor I have a good reason why not. Maybe it has to do with concerns about drowning, or it's too close to eating in a room largely made for the opposite purpose. In the end, just like our parents before us, sometimes you don't need an explanation; "because I said so" is good enough.

Handbook Tips: Do's and Don'ts

▸ Most adults break the rules at least some of the time. We cross the street in the middle of a block. We eat in bed, leave the dishes in the sink, and throw recyclables into the trash. Some of us are petty criminals, taking illegal recreational drugs or cheating on our taxes. Yet we don't want our kids to do any of these things. What to do? You can't really confess out right, at least until just before they board the plane to go to college. You certainly can't go completely straight; there's no fun in that. There's really only once choice: hide your evil ways as long as possible. If they discover that you're a secret smoker or look at pornography deny it all with a straight face. And then find a better hiding place for your stash.

▸ Like most kids, Sara's a rule follower. She won't cut in line, lie about her age to get a lower price ticket at the movie theatre or amusement park, trespass on private property, or crash a party to which she wasn't invited. I'm hoping it's just a phase from which she'll grow out.

▸ If you want your kid to wash their hands, brush and floss their teeth and clip their finger and toenails, you should do the same. A side benefit: it'll do wonders for your romantic life.

I Can Walk!

I'd have been foolish to believe that once I'd become a father I'd stop making the same mistakes I made when I was childless. But sometimes the blunders go down easier with a family.

One of my bad habits is acting without thinking things through. Before I moved in with Debbie I lived in a series of studio and one-bedroom apartments, one of which was located in San Francisco's lower Haight neighborhood, which at the time was pretty dodgy. After I'd settled in on the third floor of a Victorian walk-up, one of my downstairs' neighbors – a group of bicycle messengers – smashed every window in their apartment during a raucous party.

A few months later a friend was visiting. "Hey," he shouted, as he peered out the window to the street below, "someone's stealing my car!"

"What? Where?" I asked. He pointed to a red Toyota parked across the street. Two 20-something African-American men were sitting in its front seat.

"Come on!" I said, as I raced out the door. My friend followed me down the stairs, though he lagged farther behind than I'd have expected. Outside, I ran up to the car, and thrust my head towards the driver's side window, which was half-open.

"Get out of the car!" I shouted at the man calmly sitting in front of the steering wheel.

"What?" he responded. "This isn't your car," his voice had an edge of anger.

"No, but it's not yours either. Now get out."

"You better step back, mister."

"No, you better get out of the car," I retorted. My friend had finally made it outside, and was hovering somewhere behind me.

"Mister. This isn't your car. Your car is behind this one," the man said, with a Clint Eastwood-like snarl, gesturing towards his backseat.

I looked to where he was pointing. An identical vehicle – same color, same make and model – was parked directly behind him.

"Is that your car?" I asked my friend, my voice almost cracking. He nodded sheepishly.

I raised my hands in surrender. "I'm sorry, man, my mistake," I said to the man in the car.

"You're right, it's your mistake," he whispered fiercely. It sounded like a threat, or perhaps a promise he was making to his companion sitting next to him. He shook his head as he turned on the ignition.

I returned to my apartment, my friend tailing behind. The next day as I approached my car I saw what seemed to be blotches all over it. Someone had thrown a gallon of puke-yellow paint on its sides and roof. It cost me several hundred dollars to clean it up. I never found out who did it.

Recently, Debbie, Sara and I were waiting in an airport security line to get to our departure gate. As we piled our shoes and carry-on luggage onto the conveyor belt, an attendant pushed an older woman in a wheel chair to the front of the line. The woman jumped out of the chair, strode past the line of people wrangling their baggage, and through the metal detector portal.

"She can walk, she can walk," I said, looking at Sara, while shaking my hands in the air "Hallelujah!"

"She can walk," Sara mimicked me, smiling broadly.

"That's my fcking mother!" a large man standing behind us yelped, as he stared at the top of my head.

I turned to look at him. "I'm sorry man, I was just playing around. I meant no disrespect."

"That's my fcking mother," he grumbled. "She's got varicose veins."

"Really, I apologize."

I turned back to the conveyor belt to load the remaining bag. Sara pretended that nothing had happened. After we'd made it through security, and distanced ourselves from the aggrieved son, Debbie gave me a mischievous smile.

"I can walk!" she exclaimed under her breath.

And we did, all the way to our plane.

On our Moroccan trip, in Marrakesh, after wandering for a couple of hours in the Berber market's windy, narrow alleyways, we were lost. Our guidebook map didn't have the detail we needed to determine where we were. At first it was fun, being adrift in the *souk*, strolling past the dozens of stalls proffering camel meat, pistachios, candies, fabric, lamps, and beads that lined the twisty, narrow streets. It felt like we'd been absorbed into another world. But the sun was starting to set, and Sara was tired.

Looking for someone from whom to ask directions, I spotted an elderly man sitting in a chair in front of a small shop that sold indeterminate items. He was staring into space, as if he was watching the clouds go by. I marched up to him.

"Excuse me," I said, "Do you know how we might get to this address?"

I shoved a piece of paper in front of his face on which the name and location of our *riad* was written. The man ignored me, stared over my shoulder, down the alley behind me.

"It's Riad des Cigognes, on rue de Berim," I announced, loudly and slowly, in a mangled French accent. The man said something in Arabic. His eyes shifted upwards a bit. I looked at his face.

"I think he's blind," I said to Debbie and Sara, who were standing behind me. A younger man walked up to the elderly Moroccan, bent over him, and said something in his ear that I couldn't hear.

"Go away," the younger man said to me, making shooing motions with his hands. He turned to the elderly Moroccan and asked him something in Arabic. I backed away to my family.

"He's blind?" Sara asked.

"I think so," I said.

"You asked directions from a blind man?" Debbie asked, smiling.

"Yes, I believe I did," I responded. Sara giggled. We grabbed each other's hands, and continued to look for our hotel. It took us awhile, but we eventually found it.

Handbook Tips: Kids Say the Stupidest Things…And so do Dads

▸ When you say or do something stupid, let your wife and kid laugh at you. When they do the same, it's better to keep your mouth shut. Trust me on this one.

▸ It's possible to learn from your mistakes, but it can be funnier not to.

▸ You'll know when you've done something especially stupid, or dangerous, if, instead of laughing, someone in your family cries or yells at you. Don't do that again.

Get on the Bus

"I'm really happy!" said Sara, on the way home from school.

"Why's that?" I asked.

"Because I'm sitting next to Silvie on the bus, going to the field trip! I was talking to her at recess, and I asked her if she was sitting with anybody. She said 'no' so I asked her if she'd sit next to me, and she said 'yes.'" Sara chattered. "Jessica already asked me to sit with her on the way back," she added, cheerfully.

Starting with fourth grade – when the kids went on a three day overnight to California's Gold Country – securing friends to sit next to on the bus, and share a bunk bed with, emerged as the unspoken social challenge of the year. The stakes were high enough that the practice, invented by the students without adult prompting, was to split the trip into departure and return rides, selecting different companions for each segment. That way a popular kid could sit with twice as many friends, and a less popular one had a better chance of finding a seatmate for at least one stretch of the journey.

Sara was initially slow to understand the importance of this popularity test. In the lead-up to the Gold Country trip she only became aware that her peers were actively making seating and sleeping reservations with one another a week before departure. By that time most of her friends already had partners. She scrambled to find someone to sit with, and was unable to locate anyone with whom to share a bunk. She ended up sleeping in a single bed, "like the teachers," she explained to me afterwards. She wasn't bitter about the outcome, and it didn't much dent her innate optimism and sunny self-esteem. But she knew that she'd failed socially.

"What happens if you don't find someone to sit with on the bus," I asked, after she told me about her successful fifth grade travel plans.

"You may end up sitting next to a boy! Though I don't think the boys care so much," she added, thoughtfully.

"That wouldn't be so bad," I responded. But, since she'd already solved her immediate problems, she pretended not to hear me.

For a girl with lots of friends, but no consistent best friend – BFF – Sara's seating chart challenge reflected the next stage of her social evolution. Following the typical pattern, when she was a baby she didn't play with anybody but herself; as a toddler she shifted to "parallel play," which could be with a boy or a girl, it didn't much matter to anyone involved.

After she reached school age the stakes got higher. Children started having more focused play dates, which needed to be assiduously scheduled, and tended to revolve around specific activities: Lego, if boys were involved; playing imaginary games if it was girls. By the time Sara was six, gender differences began to materialize; by seven playing with boys, other than as a result of being thrust together at adult-dominated parties, ended.

This next stage – finding the right person to sit, or sleep, with – will unfold over a lifetime. My own strategy, which I first deployed as a shy adolescent, and stuck with into adulthood, was defensive. I'd take whoever was available on a bus, at a party, or in a classroom, and try to make the best of it. I'd even create a game out of my approach, sparking conversations with the least popular kid in school, or searching out someone who was standing alone at a party to talk with. The method has its benefits. I've met some interesting people. But I'd be lying if I said I never ended up eating next to someone at a meal, periodically glancing at another table, wishing I was seated elsewhere.

"Shoot!" cried Sara, as she was getting ready for bed the night before the field trip.

"What's wrong?" I asked.

"My teacher told us to write down six girls we'd want to share a tent with, and they'd put us into groups of four," she said.

"Uh huh," I said. "So, who did you pick?"

"Jessica, Beia...some others," Sara said, in a hurry to get to the punch line. "But for my sixth choice I put down a girl I don't like! What if I get her?"

"Why did you do that?" I asked.

"I dunno!" Sara cried. "It was a mistake!"

"I wouldn't worry about it. I'm sure your teachers will do the right thing," I said. I kept it to myself that I was proud of my daughter. It might have been a mistake, her including a "frenemy" in her list of tent mates, but I chose to think of it as unconsciously intentional. What better way to fight the peer pressure machine – and learn to get along with diversity – then to occasionally choose people you didn't like with whom to share a tent?

Handbook Tips: How to Make a Friend

▸ Well into second grade Sara employed a blunt strategy to find playmates. If she was alone in a park or schoolyard she'd walk up to pretty much any available kid and ask, "Do you want to be my friend?" sometimes deploying the variation, "Do you want to be best friends?" Most of the time her would-be companion said "yes," though many wouldn't stick, drifting off before too long. Others might stare at her stonily, or say "no." By third grade she'd learned that a full frontal friendship attack was frowned upon, and dropped the strategy. I'm sure it'll reemerge later int her life; at a toned-down level it's a pretty good approach to meeting people.

▸ As a teenager my nephew Asa deployed a variation

on my tactic when it came to finding bus mates. He'd bring a pad and pen, choose an empty row, and busy himself drawing. If the person who ended up sitting next him seemed interesting, he'd use his doodles as a conversation starter; if not he'd busy himself with his picture, signaling his own no-socializing zone.

Urban Critters

"What's that?" 10-year-old Sara asked.

It was early on a Saturday morning, and we were walking past Dolores Park, a large expanse of green in the middle of San Francisco, not far from the city's historic gay neighborhood. A chain-link fence circled the children's playground, which was being renovated. Standing hard up against the fence, facing the sidewalk where Sara's pace had slowed so she could gawk, was a 20-something man dressed only in tight leather underwear. A large metal cuff bolted his neck to the fence; his hands were behind his back, undoubtedly shackled as well. Out of the corner of my eye I could see a police cruiser pulling up.

"Um, I dunno," I said, searching for something acceptable to say. "I guess he was playing around."

"But why is he in his underwear," Sara asked, her eyes bulging towards the man. "And why is he locked up?"

"Let's go," I said tugging at her hand.

She reluctantly followed, her head twisted in the direction of the man. A pair of police officers ran across the grass towards him.

"But Daddy, what happened?"

"Maybe he was playing around with a friend, and he got hot, so he took his shirt off," I tried.

Sara looked at me suspiciously. I shrugged my shoulders, "I don't really know."

The image stuck with both us. Periodically, when we visit the park, Sara will tell one of her friends what she'd seen. She still doesn't have an explanation for what a half-naked man was doing chained to the fence surrounding her local playground. But, then again, neither do I.

"Eeew, gross," Sara yelped, as we drove by a stub of Golden Gate Park located at the western end of Haight Street, widely known as "Hippie Hollow." Over the years we'd often strolled through the area on our way to the Koret Children's Quarter, which features a carousel. The Hollow is usually choked with drifters, many of whom smell ripe, some of whom are often pulling on, or trying to sell, a joint. Since Sara prefers to walk on the low stone retaining wall that lines the Hollow's pathways, she often has to skirt past a shaggy man or two dressed in near rags who are using the wall as a bench, something she hasn't seemed to mind. Up until now.

"What?" I asked.

"That guy just vomited on the wall. That's disgusting. I'm never touching anything in that area again."

"That is kind of gross," I said.

"Those people are so filthy," Sara frowned.

I worry that Sara's urban encounters with society's more free-spirited, or down-on-their luck, members might cause her to develop prejudices against the poor or homeless. But so far that hasn't seemed to have happened. She often encourages me to give money to panhandlers, and interrogates me when I don't, wanting to know what's behind my choice to be generous, or not. She's particularly sympathetic to buskers, to whom she almost never fails to give a dollar. When an initiative appeared on our local ballot to prohibit anyone from sitting or lying on the sidewalk – which was directed, in part, at the individuals who use Hippie Hollow as their base – Sara was staunchly against it. "That's stupid," she'd say. "People should be allowed to sit on the sidewalk. Where else are they supposed to go?"

But as Sara reached adolescence her tolerance appears to be increasingly tested.

"I have an idea," Sara said, as we turned the corner away from Golden Gate Park.

"What's that," I asked.

"The City should set aside some land for the hippies to stay on. It could have bathrooms and drinking fountains. And then families could use the park more easily."

"That's not a bad thought," I said.

I knew it wasn't the last time we'd talk about this subject. And maybe that's a good thing. After all, learning how to cope with shackled naked men and bedraggled hippies is part of city living. Maybe, when's she's all grown-up, Sara will even come up with an approach to sharing public space that works for everyone. In the meantime, I'm hoping that we've reached the limits of the urban sights for which I can't provide an explanation.

Handbook Tips: Explaining Things
- ▸ Lots of things are hard to explain to a child, or even an adult. Why is America involved in wars in the Middle East? Where do bees go in winter? Why are people mean? I don't know; do you?

- ▸ It's okay to say "I don't know" in response to a complicated query, like, "why don't birds get electrocuted when they sit on electricity wires?" Or, if you've done that too much lately, try slowing down your response, and throwing in lots of multi-syllable words, like a stereotypically book-trained convict. Chances are your kid will get bored before you'll have to come up with a real answer. Though of course eventually they'll catch on, and insist that you just cop to not knowing what you're talking about.

- ▸ Once they start school the ante will simultaneously increase, and decease. You'll probably need to help them with math, grammar rules, and science – feel free to read ahead in their text books – but you can also tell them that it's their job to find the answers. Google, anyone?

Girls Only

Sara and Debbie are going through similar stages. In Sara's case, I believe scientists call it the "boys are yucky" syndrome. Syndrome symptoms include avoiding touching boys, or even brushing against them, unless it involves poking; going through the school yearbook to identify which boys are ugliest and most annoying; and occasionally comparing notes with other girls about which boys they "like-like." A little unrequited flirtation adds some spice to an otherwise monolithic wall of gender disdain.

Debbie's condition manifests similarly, though with a few notable differences. It's evidenced by girls-only vacations and nights-out; going through lists of husbands or male colleagues to identify which are least interesting and most annoying; and practicing "safe sex" by including in the group at least one, non-threatening but hilarious gay man. A little testosterone keeps things jumping; just not too much.

Being on the male-side of this divide, I'm left wondering if there's some evolutionary purpose to gender segregation. Sara is at the beginning edges of puberty; Debbie post-menopause. Perhaps an absence of fertility renders straight males useless. Or maybe there are periods in life when each of the genders can best decide who they want to be by learning from same sex interactions. Divorce rates peak in the mid-forties; is that because that's when girls need to drift back to their pre-pub roots, more interested in gossip and make-believe than whatever it is that men previously had to offer?

Ten-year-old boys seem to go through a stage of their own, which might be termed the "what's a girl?" phase. They're too busy playing sports, or poking one another, to notice that virtually the entire girl population – except a few sporty, cross-over types – don't give them no never-mind. And my mid-life male peers? Most of them seem to be returning to their own boyhood behaviors, busily chasing balls, though the goal posts are mostly defined by money.

Those who aren't are in the midst of their own pre-pubescent-like identity crises. Rather than staring at their face in the mirror in search of emerging pimples, they look for the next wrinkle. Either way, they're too absorbed in their own distractions too notice that the girls aren't paying attention to them anymore.

As for me, I grew up with three sisters, so am used to being variously the object of spirited affection and neglectful abuse, and giving back the same. And anyways, I'm too busy examining my receding hairline in the mirror, and researching hair loss remedies, to care much about what the women around me are doing.

Handbook Tips: Gender Differences

▶ Even as we evolve towards greater gender equality, differences between girls and boys remain. My experience, growing up with three sisters, and still out-numbered by the opposite sex in my adult household, is that women tend to talk and cry more and dress better than, men. Both genders seem to laugh about the same amount, though.

▶ Some new parents hope for a baby boy, others for a baby girl. In the end, though, children love is genderless.

The Daddy Handbook

"There's no such thing as a *Daddy Handbook*," Sara, said, squinting at me suspiciously.

"Sure, there is," I countered. "It's issued to every dad when they bring home their baby."

"Show it to me, then," she insisted.

"I can't," I replied, "It's for daddies' eyes only. I'd be breaking the daddy code if I let you see it."

Since Sara could talk in semi-complete sentences, I've been invoking the *Daddy Handbook* as a disciplinary tool, though I've never actually shown it to her, and, for all she knows, it doesn't exist.

"Why do I have to go to bed at 7:30?"

"Because of the *Daddy Handbook*."

"I don't want to buckle my seat belt!"

"Sorry, the *Daddy Handbook* says you have to. If you

don't, I might lose my daddy privileges."

Oddly, given my strong-willed and charmingly manipulative daughter, citing the handbook mostly works. She protests less, and with better humor, when I call it out. When she was little the book tickled her desire for a higher authority, a league of daddies who had carefully thought-out responses to murky situations. It made her feel safe. As she negotiates adolescence, her belief that the book is real has diminished, though it remains higher than her faith that the tooth fairy is anybody other than me.

It helps that I've used the handbook sparingly, and mostly for things that make intuitive sense to her, even if she doesn't like the rules: sleep, safety, and hygiene. I tried employing the handbook once to get her to do her homework, but quickly abandoned the tactic when it became clear that a book she's never seen was powerless in the face of the quite real math exercises she held in her hand.

Lately, I've had to dip into the book's more creative recesses to get her attention. A few weeks ago she refused to brush her teeth before bedtime, preferring to play with a half-deflated balloon.

"You gotta brush your teeth," I said, "it's in the *Daddy Handbook*."

She ignored me.

"Alright, then," I continued, "I'll need to call the tooth brushing guy." I could see her ears perk up.

"What tooth brushing guy?" she asked. "There's no tooth brushing guy."

"Sure, there is," I replied, "he advertises in the *Daddy Handbook*. You give him a call, and he'll come over and brush your children's teeth. He even does dogs."

"Huh," she said, still playing with her balloon, though with diminished intensity.

I'll go call him," I said. As I walked to grab my cellphone from the other room a strong wind rattled the windows. "Oh, maybe he's here already."

"No need, no need," said my daughter, rushing to the bathroom to brush her teeth.

"Maybe that wasn't him after all," I said, as I looked out the window.

But by that time my daughter, her teeth freshly scrubbed, was already in bed.

Handbook Tips: What Kind of Dad are You?

Becoming a father is an act of personal invention; you need to decide how you're going to play your role. I could have modeled my behavior after my own dad, but he was mostly emotionally and physically absent when I was growing up, consumed with earning enough money to pay for his five kids. I never went to dad school, assuming such an institution exists, and haven't found an older friend or relative to emulate. Once I became a father, though, my experiences with other dads suggested that there are lots of ways to be a dad:

▸ *Yelling dad:* This style peaked in popularity in 1972, after which the pressure of the woman's movement, stagflated economy, and anti-war demonstrations

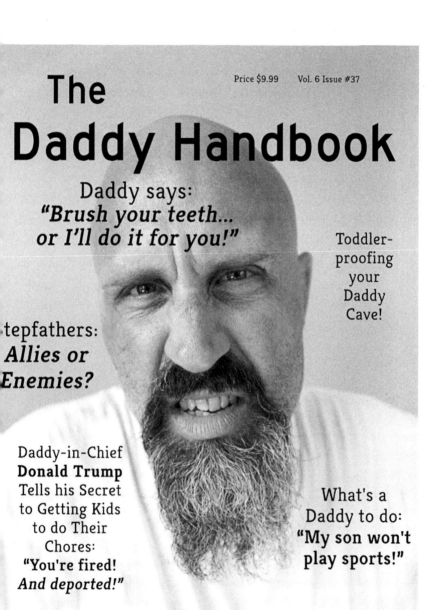

The

Daddy Handbook

Price $9.99   Vol. 6 Issue #37

Daddy says:
*"Brush your teeth...
or I'll do it for you!"*

Toddler-
proofing
your
Daddy
Cave!

tepfathers:
*Allies or
Enemies?*

Daddy-in-Chief
Donald Trump
Tells his Secret
to Getting Kids
to do Their
Chores:
**"You're fired!
And deported!"**

What's a
Daddy to do:
**"My son won't
play sports!"**

squeezed this 1950s dad model so hard that it popped. Yelling dad is known for angry, abrupt, and random outbursts, triggered by anything from spilt milk to a child's balloon accidentally hitting his head. Tends to result in tip-toeing children pre-adolescence, followed by talking-back, rebellious teenagers, with teary-eyed reconciliation usually accomplished at Yelling dad's death bed. Closely related to Alcoholic dad.

▸ *Remote dad:* Popular among academics, hedge fund managers and engineers, Remote dad – also known as "Chilly dad," and "Divorced dad" – acts as if he lives inside an invisible bubble, impervious to all forms of communication. Remote dad spends a lot of time on the computer – hand-held or otherwise – watching televised sports, and in his "man cave," which, for divorced fathers, may also be called his "apartment." Chilly dad often rears children who'll do anything to get attention, frequently producing stand-up comedians, shoplifters, and sluts.

▸ *Cool dad:* Likes to be called "daddy-o," or by his first name, cool dad makes everything seem effortless. Quickly comforts a child who has skinned her knee with an all-natural, organic, fruit popsicle, a tube of arnica, and Sponge Bob-branded bandages; always ready for a game of horseshoes, or to pick apart an old computer for parts; often wears a hat, pork-pie or otherwise. Cool dad can irritate other fathers, and tends to hang-out with the moms at school functions, which can lead to a modified version of "Divorced dad."

▶ *Sporty dad:* Always wearing Lycra, even to school socials, sporty dad is on the move, coaching teams, setting up archery targets in the back yard, and participating in iron man contests. Sporty dad often attracts a crowd of boys, and tends to forget who his actual progeny are, treating all children with the same disciplined energy. Can occasionally lead to "Fat dad" after age or injuries take their toll. Results in either athletic adults, or pasty-faced couch potatoes who don't like to leave the house.

▶ *Gay daddy:* May not actually have children, Gay daddy tends to be large and friendly, though sometimes in a threatening kind of way that you can't quite put your finger on. Gay daddy likes to be the center of attention, and is always ready with a quick opinion or fatherly advice. If married to a woman, Gay daddy tends to exhibit obsessive behavior, like ironing his underwear, or making sure the cereal boxes and cleaning products are arranged in alphabetical order. Children of Gay daddies are often well-rounded, fully-engaged adults, who prefer to live in small, homogeneous Midwestern towns.

▶ *Stay-at-home dad.* The latest in fatherhood styles, stay-at-home dad dresses casually, and can be found at school pick-up and drop-offs, cheering field-side at

kiddy athletic events, and as the sole male in mommy-dominated playgroups. Stay-at-home dads may be the fastest-growing of the daddy genres. It's a group that's still inventing itself; proud to wear an apron, but mostly to teach their children pottery making, industrial arts, or farm-to-table cooking schemes. It's too early to tell how the offspring of Stay-at-home dads will fair. They could go the way of a now virtually extinct model – Hippie-commune dad; otherwise known as "who are you?" – or, more likely, create an entirely new demographic of sensitive-hipsters.

There are of course many other styles of fatherhood, including Busy dad, Stands-to-Close dad, and Long Distance dad. My own daddy identity is still evolving, which matches with Sara's preferences. Over the years she's called me "Poppy," "Abba," "Dad," and "Daddy," each of which reflect a certain way of being, at least to her. And I'm happy to take any of those names, so long as she doesn't call me "sir."

Dancing on my Shoulders

Since Sara was born, on June 30, 2001, at 9:03 p.m., lot's has happened, both in the world, and in her world. Almost 3,000 Americans died in a terrorist attack on the East Coast. In response, the United States waged war in Afghanistan or Iraq from the time Sara was less than two years old until after she turned 11. The nation suffered through two economic downturns, the second one possibly as part of a structural shift towards permanently lower wage growth and intensifying concentrations of wealth and poverty. An African-American man was elected president, then a billionaire businessman. High- and bio-technologies reshaped the way people communicate, eat, and do business.

Closer to Sara's home, her Uncle Harvey died of Amyotrophic lateral sclerosis, leaving behind three sons under the age of 14. She moved houses four times, and schools twice.

She was within one hundred yards – though didn't actually see – a cheetah when it tracked and killed a gazelle in Tanzania. She learned how to read, write, and swim. She made new friends, and lost them. All that, and it's been less than a decade and a half.

Sara's my only child. I wish I had more, but I'm profoundly blessed that I have her. All parent-child relationships are special, but fathers and only daughters have a particularly intense connection. At least Sara and I do. And maybe it's because of that that I know, someday, Sara is going to break my heart. Just by growing up.

Traveling in Southern India roughly 13 years ago, we came across a religious ceremony, which featured more than a dozen costumed elephants, a troupe of drummers, a small crowd of dancers, and a circle of onlookers. Debbie and I walked up to the throng, two-year-old Sara perched on my shoulders, into the mass of dancers. As we got closer to the drummers, Sara started to bounce, faster, and faster, as if dancing to the music. I couldn't see her, but she felt like she was jumping for joy.

"What's she look like," I shouted over the beat to Debbie.

"She looks," Debbie beamed back, "ecstatic. I don't think I've ever seen anybody look that happy. Ever."

We held hands and danced together, the crowd swaying and smiling around us, Sara jumping on my shoulders, as if it would last forever. And whatever else happens in the world, or her world, it will for me.

Write Your Own Handbook

Every dad has a story. Here's a few exercises to get yours started. Answer the following questions by writing, uninterrupted, for 10 minutes. Try not to filter out any thoughts; let it flow!

The best thing about being a father is:
The worst thing about being a father is:
I want to tell my child(ren):
It surprised me when my daughter/son:
I was scared out of my mind when:
I bust out laughing when:
The biggest mistake I ever made as a father was:

Steven Moss lives with his awesome wife, Debbie Findling, in San Francisco's Mission Dolores neighborhood with their daughter, Sara, and dog, Lucky.